When Bright Kids Can't Learn

How New Brain Research Can Help Your Child

John F. Heath

ISBN 0-9785423-0-4
When Bright Kids Can't Learn
By John F. Heath

www.LearningTechnics.com

1-800-893-9315

Cover design: Joshi L. Haskell

First printing: April 2006
Second printing: February 2008
Third printing: January 2013

Printed in the United States of America

ACKNOWLEDGEMENTS

Many people helped make this book possible, especially the following:

- Loretta Heath, my wife and partner, who made enormous contributions to the clarity and organization of this text. She spent untold hours at the computer to bring this book to life. Thanks, Loretta!

- Sally Higley, who has been my business colleague for over seventeen years. She has never accepted the status quo. She has always taken me down the road less traveled and that has made all the difference in our research.

- Don Aslett and Carol Cartaino, who used their years of writing and publishing experience to start me out in the right direction.

- Byron Christensen, who read through my unfinished manuscript and said, "This book is needed. You should get busy and finish it."

- Mary Johnson, who shared thirty years of classroom experience with me.

- Linda Archibald, who researched and summarized large volumes of material to find the information most applicable for this book.

- Joshi Haskell, our graphics and photo guru, whom we would have been lost without.

TABLE OF CONTENTS

Note:
To protect identities of students, parents and others, some names and
case descriptions have been altered without changing the essential
reality of each case.

Foreword

Darcy C. Jack, Ed.D.

During my years as a high school reading specialist and language arts teacher, I witnessed seemingly bright kids struggling with basic learning skills. Despite devoting extra effort toward classroom strategies that stimulate fluency and reading comprehension, the "one size fits all" nature of the classroom prohibited me from adequately addressing cognitive processing deficiencies occurring at individual levels. This book does a fine job explaining why bright kids have trouble learning and offers a research founded alternative to traditional intervention.

Years ago during my doctoral pursuit, I discovered an emerging applied brain research company, Learning Technics, which focused upon a "whole brain approach" to remediating learning problems. The program is founded upon the results of brain imaging technology which revealed a co-dependent relationship between the brain's left and right hemispheres. While the left hemisphere of the brain breaks down information, the right hemisphere puts it altogether into a coherent pattern. Reading, for example, is an intricate process of decoding words while simultaneously reassembling them in an order that promotes comprehension and fluency. Within this process, the efficient reader automatically recodes graphemes (alphabetical script) into corresponding phonemes (linguistic sounds). Without this automatic visual and auditory process, word patterns are unrecognizable.

The 26-week Learning Technics program relies upon an intricate array of repetitive visual, auditory and physical exercises to remodel right and left hemispheres of the brain into processing skills that enhance the brain's capacity to perceive, process, store and retrieve information. Remediating the underlying processing problems that cause learning problems is immediately apparent in improved comprehension and memory. When the program is completed, the student continues to progress at an increasing rate because processing has become more efficient. Thus, unlike traditional tutoring programs, the progress does not stagnate at the end of the program but excels as the student continues in life.

Realizing that the true worth of a program is determined by results, I began sitting in on Learning Technics sessions. Inside the front door of the Boise office is a thick "parent testimony" book filled with words like "miracle" to describe the influence of Learning Technics on their children. As a student and teacher of the traditional education system, I was highly skeptical about these claims, as well as those made by the director and Learning Technics instructors. However, it wasn't long before I began seeing the results for myself.

A prototypical example of a Learning Technics student is 13-year old Emily, who struggled mightily with all aspects of school. The Learning Technics initial evaluation revealed severe reading comprehension problems, an aversion to reading and a despondency toward learning. Emily had hopelessly struggled with other interventions, causing her father to share Emily's opinion that further intervention was futile. Emily's mother, however, had witnessed remarkable results in her neighbor's child who had accomplished Learning Technics. The child was held back due to reading difficulty and staying on task. The father related his son's newfound ability in these areas as well as his improvement in confidence and self-esteem.

Upon entering the program, Emily and her mother worked hard during their hour-long sessions. Twelve weeks into the program, Emily's dad expressed amazement when he saw his daughter reading books on her own. The first book Emily ever completed was about a gymnast, who, like Emily, had learning difficulties in school. Because Emily was also a gymnast, she could relate to the character. She finished the book in just three days. She couldn't believe her own success. She had never read a book before because she could never understand what she was reading. "I hated reading," she told me. "I finished the series (three books) and then started reading *The Hunger Games*." Near the end of the program, Emily was beaming and couldn't wait to share her news. She subsequently received a "proficient" score on her state standardized test, which meant that she was reading on grade level. Before Learning Technics, she had always gotten a "below basic" score.

Though Emily's academic progress was remarkable, perhaps the most significant improvement occurred in her self-esteem, confidence and sense of self-empowerment. Concurrent with Learning Technics' academic objectives is their commitment to 20 Life Management Concepts, which empower the student's ability and willingness to manage their own learning process and constructive behaviors. This aspect of the program was particularly evident in Will, a 9-year-old who had been diagnosed with pervasive developmental delay and a speech impediment. Initially, while doing his Learning Technics exercises, Will would lose interest and act out. But, his mother (the trainer) persistently followed the instructor's prescribed directives. Gradually, Will's mother noticed an emerging positive attitude toward learning, others and himself. Near the end of the program, Will's standardized reading test score improved from "below basic" to "basic," and his reading fluency went from 58 words per minute to 105 words per minute. "This was huge," his mother exclaimed. "Before (Learning Technics) we weren't even in the ballpark."

Will's mother also referred to the "unexpected side effects" of Learning Technics. Because Learning Technics includes physical activities to stimulate various parts of the brain, Will's balance and coordination improved. "It blew my socks off," she said. "Will is now able to skip rope, do jumping jacks and ride a bike. Before Learning Technics, he couldn't even do a simple jumping jack." Like Emily and so many other Learning Technics students, Will acquired a disciplined focus on goal setting, whereby tasks are systematically broken into manageable pieces and success points. In this way, students learn the ability to efficiently structure their time and realize success without feeling overwhelmed.

Like fellow veteran educators who work part time at Learning Technics, I have become an ardent believer in the ability to remediate processing problems in struggling learners. But, I stop short in using words like "miracle" to describe Learning Technics. The fact is, Learning Technics is not for everyone. An evaluation is the first step in the Learning Technics process. If it is determined that the student has more than one processing weakness Learning Technics is recommended. However, in order to achieve optimum success, students and trainers must be willing to work six hours a week. Because restructuring or creating new automatic brain patterns necessitates considerable repetition and discipline, the Learning Technics process is fully dependent upon the student and trainer's diligent commitment to a challenging step-by-step process. When this program is implemented correctly, it offers huge permanent solutions to learning problems. But, it is important to recognize that the miracle many parents refer to is primarily conditioned by their loving devotion to their child. If a parent is unable or unwilling to make this commitment, Learning Technics will have limited success.

As a public educator, there are few rewards greater than turning around the life of a struggling learner. In trying to help these students, I realized the limited ability of traditional educational and tutor based programs for remediating individual processing problems, thus becoming short-term temporary fixes for long term problems. In addition to lacking the tools for correcting processing problems, they lack the capacity to psychologically connect struggling learners to a sense of self-improvement. Through Learning Technics' 20 Life Management Concepts, students learn to make constructive choices and create goals to achieve success. For this reason, I heartily recommend this book to teachers and parents of struggling learners. For me, Learning Technics has provided a sense of purpose and profound joy in helping others unlock the doors to their own success and fulfillment. It is a light in the tunnel for parents and students, providing a path for greater hope and a brighter future.

Research Summary

By Byron J. Christensen, Ed. D.

Introduction

Much has been said and written about brain based learning in the past few years. Most of the dialogue has been focused on understanding how the brain learns and teaching to each student's neurological strength, thus the statement, "Many children learn differently and therefore must be taught differently." This may be true in theory, but as all teachers know, it is next to impossible to implement in the classroom. Now new brain research has developed techniques to broaden and strengthen a student's ability to take in information more efficiently. This procedure is called Physio-Neuro Therapy. After using these neurological techniques, the student can learn effectively through the normal presentation of information in the classroom, rather than changing the presentation to meet each student's individual needs.

New Research Findings on
Which Physio-Neuro Therapy is Based

The brain is in a constant state of remodeling throughout life.

"The wonderful thing about the brain is [that it is] not a static organ; it is a constantly changing mass of cell connections that are deeply affected by experience and hold the key to human intelligence," stated Peter Huttenlocker, a neurobiologist from the University of Chicago. Ronald Kotulak, author of *Inside the Brain*, commented, " This ability of the brain to rewire itself, grow new parts for damaged cells, and even make new cells–its 'plasticity,' in scientific jargon–was thought to be impossible only a few years ago. Brain cells, medical students were taught, were hardwired like so many computer transistors. Once they burned out, that was the end." (Kotulak, 1996)

The strongest single factor affecting the remodeling is mental stimulation. (McEwen, 1995)

"The most important thing is to realize that the brain is growing and changing all the time. It feeds on stimulation and it is never too late to feed it," observed Rockefeller University's B. S. McEwen. Recent research shows that proper stimulation affects such brain functions as: **(1) Language** – Mothers who talk to their children frequently help their offspring develop better language skills than mothers who seldom communicate with their young. **(2) Vision** – Good vision is essential to stimulate the development of cells that are responsible for interpreting visual stimulus. Surgeons must remove visual-blocking cataracts from infants to ensure normal development of the visual areas of the brain. (Restak, 2001) **(3) Brain Power** – Research studies show that IQs of youngsters born in poverty, or those born prematurely, can have their IQs significantly increased by exposure to words, toys, proper parenting and other types of stimulation. **(4) Touch** – Premature infants who are actively held and cuddled are physically stronger and more alert than those in isolated incubators. **(5) Education** – "The best time to learn foreign languages, math, music, and other subjects is between one and about twelve years of age." (Kotulak, 1996)

An individual's mental processes may not develop at the same rate as his/her body.

As a child's body grows and develops, neurological development does not always keep pace with the body. There is a wide range of developmental norms. The needed neurological circuits can be underdeveloped in critical areas needed for learning. When this occurs, the child struggles academically. Let's use as an example the skill of concentration (the ability of the mind to capture information being taught). As an infant, our ability to concentrate is very limited. As we mature, the ability to concentrate and keep our attention on incoming information becomes stronger. However, this development doesn't always keep pace with the chronological age of the body, thus a child of ten might have the concentration level of an eight-year-old. When this child is placed in a classroom of his peers, it is like putting a child of eight in a ten-year-old environment and expecting him to succeed. (Sousa, 2001)

All brains have an inventory of juvenile cells. (Albert, 1995)

These cells can move and permanently attach themselves to areas of weakness during specific brain-based exercises, thus permanently improving performance. "Synaptic connections, the telephone lines that allow brain cells to communicate and to learn new things, are normally overproduced in newborn brains. Mental stimulation during early childhood activates brain cells to organize synaptic connections into networks for processing new information and setting down memory. These networks are essential for such skills as language and thinking." (Kotulak, 1996)

Identifying and filling learning needs in a proactive way is essential to motivation in learning and to the maintenance of positive self-image.

William T. Greenough, a pioneering psychologist and cell biologist at the University of Illinois, exposed rats that had previously been kept in a sterile environment to one full of toys, varied foods, exercise equipment and playmates. In a short time, they were found to have 25 percent more brain connections than those that remained in the poor environment. Craig Ramey of the University of Alabama found the same thing happened to children when placed in enriched environments. In fact, Ramey tested these children twelve years later and found they had significantly higher IQ scores than the control group. PET scans, which measure brain activity, also showed that the stimulated minds were more active and efficient than those of the control group. (Ramey, 1992)

Early intervention in treating learning difficulties is crucial. (Ramey, 1992)

Martha Pierson, a neurobiologist, said, "It's just phenomenal how much experience determines how brains get put together." If you fail to develop the neurological circuitry needed for effective learning early on, you are in big trouble. Without intervention and proper treatment, an individual can face a lifetime of academic struggles.

A person is born with a multiplicity of brain cells. What the brain can do depends basically on how the brain is used and stimulated. " It is the ultimate use-it-or-lose-it machine. And it is eager to learn new skills. The ability of the brain to form abstract thoughts, for instance, is now seen as a consequence of the brain's learning to read." (Kotulak, 1996)

Two Phases of Learning

There are two phases in the learning process. The first phase is the academic phase. This is the phase in which the student is introduced to scholastic information (reading, spelling, math, etc.) Schools, tutors, and parents do this work.

The second phase is not so well understood, but is equally important. It is the neurological phase of learning. This is the phase in which the student's mind must take in the information being taught and process it. It is during this phase that "learning" takes place for the student. This is the phase in which one deals with such processes as concentration (how your mind captures information), visual memory (how you remember what you see), auditory memory (how you remember what you hear), and many other processes essential for learning. Physio-Neuro Therapy deals exclusively with this phase to strengthen the student's ability to learn.

Physio-Neuro Therapy is a highly structured and sequential series of neurological activities that are designed to stimulate and strengthen poorly developed circuits that have made learning difficult. These activities create managed overloads, which strengthen weaknesses in neurological pathways. The managed overloads create a need for juvenile brain cells, which attach themselves to the weak circuits, thereby turning weakness into strengths.

Concerns Addressed by Physio-Neuro Therapy

The following concerns are addressed in this program: Dyslexia, hyperactivity, ADD (Attention Deficit Disorder), poor reading or comprehension, difficulty remembering, poor concentration/short attention span, difficulty following directions or sequencing information, inability to complete tasks, poor self-image, directional problems, and hearing discrimination problems.

The technology and treatments discussed in this book are based on the newest brain research. This is the "new wave" of the future, and is not readily known to the public. Since twenty percent of the population (one of every five people) has difficulty mentally processing some kinds of information, there is a great need for Physio-Neuro Therapy.

$$\text{1}$$

Pinpointing Learning Problems Early

It was early fall and school had been in session for about a week. Jim, a caring parent in his mid-thirties, asked a neighbor to be sure his son, Brent, got on the bus the next morning as Jim had an early meeting. Brent was a third grader this year and Jim hoped this year would be better. His son had seemed so bright in his earlier years but, when he reached school age, everything seemed hard for him. Over the past two years things had become progressively worse and his dislike of school had increased.

About 9:00 a.m., a call came into Jim's office from his neighbor. "Brent missed the bus this morning," she said in a worried voice. "He was playing with the other children—and then he was gone."

Jim went straight home and, as he entered the house, he called for Brent. When there was no answer, he went from room to room still calling Brent's name, with no response. He went outside, walking around the house, calling without success.

Jim got in the car and began slowly driving around the neighborhood. As he continued to look for Brent, he became more concerned. Where could he be? What could have happened? After a thorough search of the neighborhood, Jim returned home. Perhaps he had missed Brent somehow.

He began going from room to room again. As he moved through the house, he heard muffled sounds that seemed to come from upstairs. He went upstairs and listened. There it was again. The sound appeared to be coming from the boy's bedroom, but there was no one there. The noise came again—from the closet. Jim slid open the door and there, under a blanket, was Brent. Brent was crying and between sobs he stammered, "Dad I can't—I can't go to school. I try, Dad, but I'm too dumb. Everyone finishes their work and I—I have to stay in every day because I'm slow!"

Jim's mind rushed to find the right words but nothing came. He knew Brent had to go to school, but something had to change. Could he expect more from the school? As a parent, could he do more? What about Brent? Jim knew he was bright; at least he seemed to be. What could he do to help him?

All parents of struggling students are frustrated. Like Jim, they care deeply but don't know what to do. Events like Brent's refusal to go to school keep bringing the problem to the forefront. Sometimes the problem seems to go away but, like a pesky rash, it keeps coming back. The symptoms can be quite different, but the story always has a familiar ring.

Not long ago I received a telephone call. A quivering voice said, "I've heard you can help poor students—is that true?" "Tell me about the problem you are trying to solve," I responded. "My son, Matt, is in the sixth grade," Laura began. "He has always struggled with learning even though he is bright (he can take anything apart and fix it, for instance). However, from the work he brought home and from parent/teacher conferences, I knew things were not going well at school. When questioned, the teachers were always kind and reassuring saying that he would mature and things would be okay. 'You're just a nervous mom,' they suggested. 'He will be fine.'"

"Soon he was two years behind in reading and math. Finally the school placed him in resource classes to give him 'special help.' They had used their best effort and he was still at the bottom of his class. The only thing to do was to lower expectations and manage him through the system. The objective seemed to be to keep him moving through the grades regardless of his academic progress.

"Now he is angry, unwilling to try, and is associating with at-risk kids."

Her voice cracked. There was silence. Then she went on.

"After six years, I know the school doesn't have the answers. I don't think I can keep him in school through graduation. I'm afraid I am going to lose him."

In some fashion this drama is played out in every classroom in America. The problem generally surfaces early in a student's education. Schools don't seem to be too concerned at first. They often associate slow learning with a lagging rate of maturity and assume time will take care of the problem. This is true for about thirty percent of such students; but for most, the problem persists.

Often public education is slow to move on such difficulties. They teach to the majority of the students who are average in learning ability, leaving the strong and weak to fend for themselves. For students with minor learning problems, tutoring can be helpful. For more challenging difficulties, however, such help does little. The use of tutoring with these students is like a tire with a slow leak. You must keep filling the tire with air—keep tutoring—to keep things rolling.

Most parents and teachers collaborate early on to assist a struggling student. They develop various means to support and communicate with each other. This is helpful, although burdensome for both parties. The results can range from the student slipping further behind, to his managing to keep even with his classmates as long as tutoring continues. As time passes with marginal results, the burden weighs heavier and the vigor of the effort lessens. Other demands get in the way. For parents it may be helping other family members with homework or chauffeuring them to music lessons or sports activities—as well as the demands of earning a living. For the teacher, there are thirty other students all with individual needs, as well as parents who are pressing for their share of the teacher's time.

(2)

The Lifelong Shadow of Learning Problems

A middle-aged man came to my office seeking help for his seventh grade son. As we talked, the conversation turned to his own difficulties in learning. He said his first memory was as a first grader. The teacher gave each child a small box filled with single letters printed on square pieces of stiff paper. Each student was to take these letters and put them in order to create the alphabet. As Bill worked at the task, he noticed that by the time he had the first few letters laid in order, most of the other students were half finished. It seemed to him that some of the letters were missing in his box. He leaned over and whispered to the child across the aisle, "Do you have an extra D? My box has no D's." His neighbor looked over at his pile of letters and picked up a D saying, "Here's one." Things like this happened over and over, day after day.

"I still remember how hard I looked for those letters," Bill mused. "They just weren't there! The children around me were so smart. They would finish the alphabet and I could only get six or seven letters. My teacher was an older lady with fiery red hair and a chalky white face. When she saw my work, her face would turn as red as her hair and the veins would stand out on her forehead and neck as she yelled at me. I didn't know what she said. I was so frightened I couldn't think.

"The second grade was much easier. My teacher was a young woman doing her first year of teaching. Looking back, I think she had no idea what to do with me. She kept me busy watering the plants in the room, sharpening everyone's pencils, running errands for her, and passing out and gathering up students' papers. Ms. Willard told my parents I was doing fine. She said I was a hard worker and got along well with others. My parents would frequently ask me how I liked school and Ms. Willard. I always had good things to say because the pressure was off and this teacher never yelled at me.

"Mrs. Woodland, my third grade teacher, was a retired principal and had taught for many years. She recognized that I was not learning and hadn't been from the start. I was probably two years or more behind. The only exception was math. I could do grade level equations and story problems if someone would read them to me. I could hardly read or spell.

"Workbooks were used for reading and spelling. These workbooks went along with a series of reader textbooks. We were given a daily assignment of a few pages in each workbook. I can't put into words how it felt to try to do that work. I couldn't read the instructions. I couldn't read the sentences in which I was to fill in the blanks." His eyes became red and tears welled up with the intense distress of the situation being relived thirty years later.

"I sat at my desk looking around," he continued. "Everyone was busily working, and I didn't know how to start. I looked at what others were doing and began to try and copy their work, hoping I wouldn't be noticed. I knew copying was cheating, but I felt I had no choice. Some students would see me looking at their work and cover it with their hand. Sometimes they would tell the teacher I was copying. She would say, 'Bill do your own work.' She seldom got mad at me. I think she knew I couldn't do the work and she was doing the best she could to help. Often, on the playground, I was called a copycat, dum-dum, and even worse.

"Every minute in the classroom was tense. I knew at any time I could be asked to do something I couldn't do. I would be forced to fail again in front of my friends. There was no way to protect myself.

"Mrs. Woodland would practice oral reading by going around the room, row by row. Each student would read a paragraph. I would count ahead to find the part I would be reading. I would read it over as many times as I could before it was my turn, hoping I could struggle through with minimum embarrassment. Invariably, however, she would have someone read two paragraphs, which would force me to stammer through an unfamiliar section. There was no way to win.

"At the conclusion of the third grade, it was determined that I could not begin to function in the fourth grade; so, I repeated third grade. The second time through was a little easier than the first time. All the earlier problems and frustrations returned, however, in the fourth grade. As the years went on, I had to explain repeatedly why I was in a particular year of school, but a year ahead getting my driver's license and other age related occurrences."

Many studies now show that holding a student like Bill back a grade does not improve future performance and it creates social difficulties. Kindergarten and first grade may be an exception if mental and social maturity seem to be lagging. At these young ages, the stigma of repeating a grade is socially less painful and time occasionally solves the underlying learning problems.

The next few years for Bill were not any better. The frustrations accumulated and he began to show hostility on the playground. He was large for his age; children who made fun of him in the classroom would get payback on the playground. Of course, he visited the principal's office often, and students' parents would call his parents complaining about altercations involving Bill.

"I began to fake sickness before and during school," Bill recalled. "Headaches and stomachaches worked. I could bring tears of pain at will. I would lay my head down on my desk and begin to cry. The teacher would ask me what was wrong. When I told her I was sick, she would send me home. I would sit on top of a hill not far from school and when I saw children crossing the road below, I knew school was out and it was time to go home.

"I was privately tutored for years with little improvement. Finally, in desperation, my parents pulled me out of the seventh grade and sent me to work with Mrs. Roberts, a learning problems specialist. She lived fifty miles away, which required a one hundred mile train ride every day. The first day she asked me 'Which do you like best, airplanes or horses?' I told her airplanes, so she pulled out a third grade book about airplanes and asked me to read a page. I thought it was a little childish, but I could read it easily. She said, 'Take this book with you and read it on the train.' I had never read a book in my life. I didn't understand how anyone could read books. It was too hard! You had to keep asking someone to read words for you or skip them. In either case you couldn't understand what you were reading. What was the use?

"This time, I read fifty pages on the way home and the whole book of two hundred fifty pages that week. Now it felt good carrying around a book and reading it as I ate my lunch like the smart kids did. The time I spent with Mrs. Roberts gave me the notion that I could read if I had the right books. There was information in books that was interesting and sometimes funny. I began pushing myself to try to read higher-grade-level books and slowly I became a better reader. However, to this day I don't read for enjoyment, only for information. And I never read to others.

"Throughout high school I was a D+ student. My stronger classes were math, physics, chemistry and geology. I had great difficulties with English, literature, history, geography and Spanish. Just prior to graduation, the guidance counselor called each senior student into his office to discuss his or her future. When it was my turn, Mr. Scott asked what my future plans were. I told him I planned to go on to college because that was what all my friends were doing. He said I would never make it there. He advised me to select a trade; something I liked to do. I was working in the bakery in a supermarket and had worked there most of my high school years. I could make many of the items produced by the bakery, so it seemed a natural trade for me to pursue. I didn't have to read or spell, and the math was easy. They agreed to make me a journeyman baker and pay me forty percent more than I was making. It was nice to have money, although I felt that I was being pigeon holed while my friends were moving ahead with their lives. But I believed I wasn't very smart and this seemed my lot in life.

"After a year at the bakery, I was sure I couldn't do this kind of work for the next forty years; so, against Mr. Scott's advice, I entered college. Perhaps I could learn enough to get out of the bakery, and I felt better telling people I was going to college. My first semester was harder than I had imagined. I failed to get a two-point grade average and automatically went on probation. This meant that if I didn't get a two-point the next semester, I was out. One semester later I was, indeed, out. Mr. Scott was right.

"The university enrollment policy stated that if a student flunked out while on probation, they could stay out one semester and then re-enroll. Upon reinstatement, the student must maintain a two point GPA or higher or they would be permanently expelled. I had one more chance and I took it. I knew I had to do things differently or I was going to flunk out again. I had to make this opportunity count.

"I was interested in business, but freshmen and sophomores were not allowed to take any meaningful business classes. I researched the registration system and planned how I could beat the system and register for upper division classes. The plan worked, and I got four C's. That meant I could go for another semester. Then I got four more C's and another semester. I never thought of graduating, which seemed impossible. Finally after three and a half years at the university, the thought crossed my mind that maybe I could graduate! I added up my credits, checked requirements, and it was indeed possible! A year and a half later, after much manipulation and tenacity, I graduated. I had learned manipulation through the years in order to survive within the educational system. I was born with tenacity.

"Since graduation, I have used these two traits every day to propel myself in the business world. It wasn't so much a choice as an absolute necessity. By forty-two I was president of a twenty-five million-dollar construction company. It seemed to others that I was doing well. To me, I was always one step from disaster. I had created a façade of confidence, organizational management and financial control. No one knew the truth. I had surrounded myself with good people who were strong in areas where I was weak. I had a secretary who could write and spell. I would tell her what to write and she fashioned it into a professional document every time. I had a great attorney who would walk me through contracts. He told me what they said and what problems might be lurking in each. I worked with quality architects who designed successful projects and followed them through to completion. The general contractors I chose were able to supervise the subcontractors and bring the projects in on budget.

"Even with all this protection I had built for myself, I was not safe. I worked for the chairman of the board of a large savings and loan. He called me weekly to check on the status of the current project. On one of his weekly calls, I mentioned some bad press we had received in the local paper. He said, 'Read me the story.' I told him it was rather lengthy and I would send it to him. He replied, 'I have time, read it to me.' I said, 'No, let me send it to you.' 'Read it!' he curtly insisted. I was stuck.

"Beads of sweat began to appear on my forehead as I struggled to read the article. As the stress heightened, my reading became more labored. I misread words and had to correct myself. Sometimes I misread the whole sentence, forcing me to repeat it. There were long hesitations as I tried to decode words that wouldn't come. It was terrible. I finished the piece and he hung up. My stomach churned for the next few days. He never spoke of that afternoon nor did I, but he knew and I knew that I was less capable than he had thought."

This is not just Bill's story. This is the story of millions of people across the country and around the world. The specifics may differ, but the tone and sequence are the same. Each of us has weaknesses that surface early in our lives and we continue to deal with them. Having a few weaknesses is common, but if they are deep or many, they affect us for a lifetime. Like Bill, we learn to live with them, work around them, and compensate for them; but they are always there, lurking in the background, ready to come out at the most inopportune time creating embarrassment and frustration. They act as an anchor preventing forward motion. The problem does not go away.

Even when students are extremely bright and can't be discouraged, they may still have trouble in school. Bre was such a student. Prior to starting school, her mother said she was quick to learn and seemed to have a stubborn streak. She would often try to do things that were beyond her years. When she was told that something was too hard, stop trying, she would belligerently ignore the advice and try harder. This unusual aggressiveness had a great influence on her ability to educate herself in spite of major learning problems. For years she reversed letters and sounds, *b-d, p-q, was-saw*, and *icook* for cookie.

Bre was strong in math, but reading was very difficult. For years, she would refuse to read because it was so hard and embarrassing. The only book she read cover to cover during twelve years of school was *Of Mice and Men.*

Bre was also socially different, and difference in school is not good. Struggling students find it very difficult to respond like other students because they don't have the same mental processing tools, thus they are forced to do things differently. They pay a heavy price for non-conformity. Bre couldn't follow a conversation, thus her comments were often irrelevant. Coordination was a problem, particularly the timing of body movements. Her movements were not smooth, so the playground was no escape for Bre. By the third grade her mother could see that Bre had great potential, but the school did not know how to work with her to bring it out. Anger flared at a number of parent/teacher conferences. Her mother and father felt the problem was with the educational system. No one seemed to understand how bright she was and how hard she was trying

After twelve years of intense effort by Bre, day after day, and constant support by her parents, she graduated from high school above many of her classmates who had made fun of her through the years, and she became an accomplished cellist—pretty remarkable for someone with poor rhythm.

By high school graduation, however, she was completely exhausted. She had nothing left—a consequence that often occurs in such cases. Burnout can occur at any time. These people feel that they have given education their best shot. They know that others have done as well or better with much less effort. It is obvious to them that they are not smart enough to go further. It is such a tragedy when great potential burns out. Restarting such a person is difficult, but it can be done.

Bre is now a junior pre-med student and is succeeding with only reasonable effort. This was made possible by seven months in a program called Physio-Neuro Therapy at Learning Technics, Inc.

$$\textcircled{3}$$

Neuroscientists Have Good News for You

For most of the past century, the mind was referred to as a "black box." It was the most mysterious three pounds of matter known to man. Only a few years ago, medical students were still taught that the mind is like a bank of computer chips. If the components are not assembled correctly or parts are damaged, you are stuck with "defective merchandise." This was called the "hardwired" theory. The crux of this theory was that if early brain development is not adequate, you are out of luck.

Today, the black box has been unlocked and neuroscientists are able to peer inside. Although the view is not perfect, what they are seeing is astonishing and the "hardwired" theory is being tossed out as brain research undergoes a mammoth revolution. It is now known that the brain can rewire itself, grow new cells to replace damaged cells, reroute pathways where blockage occurs and develop new networks to make performance stronger and easier. Neuroscientists call this phenomenon "plasticity," something that was thought to be impossible only a few years ago. Because of the brain's great plasticity, it is constantly changing cell connections and remodeling itself. This remodeling is dramatically affected by our ongoing experiences. These experiences contain the key to improving the way the brain handles information.

If there is a glitch in early brain development, these problems are usually detected by parents and teachers. Everyone recognizes there is something wrong, but may not understand that these problems are caused by weak neurological development. The symptoms of poor reading, spelling or math are often addressed, but the success rate of tutorial programs is limited because the root of the difficulty, weak neurological development, remains. New research, however, offers great hope for children and adults who struggle with these problems—a number estimated to be one out of five individuals in the United States.

Sensory-rich exercises targeted to the specific weak neuro-pathways will greatly increase neuro-connections and thereby increase the efficiency of the brain in handling information. Much like push-ups or sit-ups can strengthen physical muscles, these exercises can strengthen neurological connections and "power up" weak processes.

They can push neurological buttons that can reshape the brain. These amazing buttons are the senses of vision, hearing, and body movement. Speaking of such exercises, Paula Tallal of Rutgers University (1994) indicated that children who were unable to understand speech at normal speed were, after specific exercises and training, able to comprehend speech at a normal or above normal speed in a relatively short period of time. The networking in the brain that handles this type of information was strengthened as a result of the exercises and training making it possible for the children to process auditory information more efficiently.

"That's quite amazing," said Tallal. "It's very hopeful because it suggests that for whatever reason these children are impaired—and end up with language and reading problems—it's fixable." This improvement appears to be permanent.

As exciting and potentially life changing as this research may be, these results are often hidden under mountains of scientific data. Rarely are findings like these dispersed to the general public or even to other researchers. If they are published, it is in periodicals aimed at researchers within a specialized field. The concepts, terms, and vocabulary are often difficult for an outsider to understand.

Even though individual findings can awe neuroscientists within a specific area of study, when these findings are combined with findings from other fields, dynamic transformation of existing knowledge and practice takes place. Unfortunately, researchers tend to stay in their own fields; thus the pooling of knowledge is not common.

Most neuroscience research is done in a setting far from the day-to-day world. There can be a long lag between new finds and widespread practical use. The path of doing the research, combining it with other findings, and converting all this information into material that can be readily used and understood is a long and difficult road indeed.

4

A Solution is Born

In 1988, a company called Learning Technics took on this challenge. Sally Higley and I were the founders. We set two goals: 1) to discover why some seemingly bright people struggle with learning; and 2) to find out what can be done to permanently improve their performance.

I had struggled with reading, spelling and grammar for years. I had good parents who were concerned about my education. I remember my father sitting with me while I tried to find all the "that's," "there's," or "them's" on a page. My father would give me a penny for every one I could find and take a penny away for every one I missed. (My monetary gains were usually dismal.) Sometimes we would read the same story several times because it was easier for me to read the second and third time. My father would get so bored he would begin to look around the room instead of following along with the reading. Soon I would be reciting the story and looking around the room, too. I found it much easier to memorize the story than to read it.

As time went on, there were many tutors. They managed to keep me from failing, but their continual help was essential. I hated feeling dumb. Sometimes the frustration was so great that it would bring me to tears. Even as an adult, these problems continued to surface.

When my eight-year-old son, Trent, began to experience some of the same difficulties, I knew the frustrations that were lurking at every turn because I had been down that road myself. Trent's teachers said, "He just needs a little extra help." But I knew that tutoring was not the answer. I had been tutored to death and school had still been a struggle. I was driven to find a better path for Trent.

This quest led me to Sally Higley, who had been searching for years to find out why her bright teen could not read. She had exhausted all that the educational system had to offer without success and had been investigating a number of programs and techniques outside standard educational practices. Many of these approaches seemed weird and unconventional, but that didn't bother her. She was not going to leave one stone unturned. Sally and I found common ground in our mutual passion to help our children and also help others facing the same challenges. We decided to create an applied research company, which would conduct research in the real world as opposed to the laboratory. We named this company Learning Technics and created an advisory board of experts from the fields of medicine, psychology, psychiatry, education and sociology. All the members of the board agreed to serve without compensation because they were so excited at the prospect of what might be accomplished. None declined the request to serve. Everyone had high hopes.

Sally, the board and I began to accumulate information concerning learning problems. We found a broad range of material with differing thoughts and little consensus. The goal was to find out what was currently known and, with this in hand, form a foundation from which to start.

The educational material discovered was extensive, but only marginally helpful. Even in the field of special education, where people were highly trained to deal with learning problems, the answers were sparse. The data suggested that these hard working experts, with twice the funding that is available for regular students, were successful in returning students to the mainstream of education only about 30% of the time. A few programs would move struggling students forward; however, these programs had to be continuous or the improvements would slip away. They did not produce the permanent solution Learning Technics was seeking.

Initially, the main query revolved around teaching methods where the question was: *Why did traditional teaching methods, which seemed to be successful for 80% of the students, not work for the remaining 20%?* It became clear that teaching, in general, was adequate. If the teaching was sufficient, the only remaining possibility was that the difference in performance was caused by the struggling students' inability to turn this teaching into learning.

This was a major breakthrough. The teaching within education was not the problem. ***The problem was that these students lacked the ability to effectively turn teaching into personal learning.*** This revelation totally changed the direction of our research. The members of the Learning Technics team began to look at the student instead of the teacher or the materials. The next query naturally was: *Why couldn't the students effectively capture teaching and turn it into learning?* To answer this question, we began to look at how the brain takes in and processes information. At first, the data was overwhelming. The brain seemed so complicated and the knowledge available was not user friendly. However, with time, a basic understanding emerged about information processing. Simply stated, the mind handles information in a consistent way. Even though there are many options available, the mind chooses the process that will utilize its strengths and avoids using processing channels that are weak. This selection is made with little or no conscious thought on the part of the individual. If, however, the task at hand demands the use of a particular brain process that is weak, performance will falter. This is the plight of bright children (and adults) who struggle with learning. As an applied research company, the task of Learning Technics was to find out how to strengthen these weaknesses in order to eliminate the difficulties.

We anxiously awaited publication of new neuro-research that dealt with learning problems. By analyzing existing and new research, Learning Technics was able to put together enough components to create a basic program that was designed to strengthen the way one's mind converts teaching into learning. The next step was the testing of this program.

The first students to try this new approach were students who had been pushed through almost every remedial program known to education with minimal success. Their parents were desperate and ready to try any new approach that carried a glimmer of hope.

One of Learning Technics first students was Amanda. Although she hadn't had a nurturing beginning, she had been adopted by caring parents who tried to make up for her poor start in life. Her adoptive mother said she had been small and physically fragile when she came to live with them. She grew into a healthy, happy child, but seemed slow in her development in some areas. By the time she was well into the first grade, the problems were obvious. She was a challenge at home and at school. She couldn't follow even the most simple classroom rules such as staying in her seat. She was always talking about something, anything that popped into her head. She was so distracting in the classroom that the teacher was beside herself as to what to do with her. Amanda would learn some things quickly, but would forget almost as quickly. In spite of these difficulties, she was a charming, likable, and seemingly intelligent child.

Amanda had been identified early on as a slow learner and placed in a program called Head Start to prepare her for school. While in the first grade, she began participating in a program designed for *"at risk"* children called Title I, which was offered at her school. Next, she was referred to the school resource program. None of these programs made marked improvements in either her behavior or her learning difficulties. By the time Amanda and her parents came to Learning Technics, they were frustrated and desperate to find a solution. Her mother said: "You are our last hope. We've pursued every resource available, even some very unorthodox programs. If this doesn't work, Amanda is lost!"

Amanda worked hard and completed the course. A year later, in a follow-up conversation, her mother reported that Amanda was doing quite well and that, of all the approaches they had tried, "Learning Technics was, by far, the best use of our time and money."

At this time, Learning Technics was only in the beginning stages of research. Other students followed, all with challenging profiles. As the first students finished the course of instruction, some children made breathtaking improvements and everyone's spirits soared. Others made less than hoped for gains—which sometimes elicited questions about the validity of our work. However, each astounding success was a sign that the program was on the right track. The researchers at Learning Technics analyzed student performance and continued to refine the techniques. We kept in contact with previous students to determine if success had been maintained.

Through it all, we continued to analyze the latest developments in brain research as they might relate to learning problems. Every few months, exciting finds would surface shedding light on perplexing problems. This flow of new information brought about constant change and adjustment to fine-tune our methodologies. Though it was obvious that we were moving in the right direction, we knew that the outcome for each and every student had to be positive and predictable.

Eventually a new evaluation was designed that would work on the simple principle that, given a choice in doing a task or activity, a person will always use his/her strengths and shy away from using the weaker processes. This tendency creates a very informative evaluation of the person's mental processing strengths and weaknesses, which directly relates to academic strengths and weaknesses.

The new evaluation was an enormous success. It identified the major weaknesses in the student's neurological processes that cause learning problems. Some of these processes are: *concentration, conceptualization, pattern matching, sequencing, directionality, process synchronization, spatial reasoning, learning style preference, visual tracking, visual convergence, peripheral-vision acuity, cross brain communication, auditory discrimination, auditory memory, short/short term memory (remembering for a few seconds), short term memory (retaining things for several days), long term memory, visual memory, and skimming/detailing processing preference.*

The most enlightening result of the new testing was the realization that most individuals who suffer from learning difficulties usually have weakness in several areas. *All of these weaknesses must be addressed to improve learning in a meaningful way.*

This new vision made clear that to be consistently successful, the techniques would have to treat a wide range of problems. We decided to initially focus on and research those weaknesses that most commonly occur in problem learners. With this focus, the program—now called Physio-Neuro Therapy Training—was refined and improved as new pieces were fit into the "learning problems" puzzle. Consequently, the outcome of intervention became more predictable, more consistent. This new approach and the direction it gave translated into marked improvement in results.

$$\text{(5)}$$

The Unknown Second Phase of Learning

Learning problems are widely misunderstood because there is generally a poor perception of the learning process. This process has two major and equally important components. The first phase of learning is the academic phase where we are exposed to small bits and pieces of information that are taken in through our senses to be processed by our mind. This academic phase is most often associated with various forms of teaching and tutoring.

Teaching: The First Phase of Learning

Teachers have a great deal of latitude in running their classrooms, thus their approaches to teaching the same material can be substantially different.

Some teachers primarily lecture. These teachers are called auditory teachers. They find this method easiest for them because they have a strong auditory ability. Students who learn best by hearing information will do well in this setting, while other students will not fare as well.

Some teachers are visual people. They like to do a lot of reading and writing in their class. Charts, graphs, and diagrams seem like the clearest way to disperse information to the class. There will be a group of children who will find this format effective and engaging. These children are visual learners like the teachers. Other students will feel the class is difficult or boring because they are not strong visual processors.

A few teachers are kinesthetic. They love to take in and disperse information physically. Their classes are characterized as education in motion with many hands-on activities. These teachers are often industrial art and physical education instructors. This type of class can be maddening for students who learn best by seeing or hearing information.

The teacher controls the dispersement of information within the classroom. He or she determines the speed of instruction, the sequence in which the information is given, decides when the students understand enough to move on and what is adequate class discipline, etc. Many students are able to handle these variables year after year and do well.

Other students falter to varying degrees. Parents will jump in to help, trying to follow the lead of the school and reinforce what is being taught there. Schools frequently have supplemental programs for slower moving students such as *Success for All, Reading Recovery, Star Reading,* and *Accelerated Reading.* There are many programs and methods in use.

The integration of state and school district guidelines, teachers' adaptation of this material, their preferred teaching method, and the use of any special programs for struggling students vary greatly from classroom to classroom. *However, in all cases, the function of education—whether it takes place in a classroom, is provided by a private tutor or by parental help—is to dispense information and nothing else.*

The Critical Second Phase of Learning

The second phase of learning is called the neurological phase. This component is critical to learning, but is poorly understood by educators and not at all understood by the general public. In this phase, our mind must internalize or process incoming information as it is received through our senses. This is where the product of learning is produced. *The efficiency of this neurological processing is the key to a lifetime of success—not only in school, but also in all aspects of our lives.* Our mind processes or internalizes this incoming information from before birth until death, yet most of us have no idea how our mind really works.

Not long ago, I met with the Board of Directors of a large juvenile rehabilitation facility. These people directed the teaching and counseling of at-risk kids. They wanted to know what they could do differently to teach these students who had fallen between the cracks. This board was composed of highly educated people including many with PhD's. During the presentation, I asked a board member to explain how she remembered telephone numbers. This woman—who had a master's degree in education, was a retired teacher, and now a state senator—responded to the question with a blank look. To clarify, I elaborated, "What process does your mind use to remember phone numbers?" Her response was the same, except now she was visibly uncomfortable. She obviously had no idea how her mind remembered telephone numbers.

I then asked her if she could see a picture of the numbers in her mind. She said, "No," but I could see others sitting around the large table whose eyes lit up. Next I asked if she remembered the numbers by recalling a pattern on the telephone keypad. Again nothing seemed to register with her, but others in the room smiled and nodded. Then I asked if she remembered the number by recalling the number in a rhythmic sequence of sounds, saying each number in her mind as she dialed. Her eyes sparkled as she said enthusiastically, "Yes, that's what I do!"

Then, as I began to quiz others as to how their minds remembered telephone numbers, all were excited as they identified which of the options they used. A few used a combination of methods. This new understanding was enlightening to everyone as mental operations became a little clearer. Even more amazing to the group, however, was the fact that our individual minds often do even the simplest of tasks differently. Here was a group of highly educated people who had no idea how their minds accomplished a common, simple task that they performed many times each day; nor did they recognize that different individuals often use different processes to accomplish the same task—processes that relate directly to our individual processing strengths and weaknesses.

Mental development unfolds differently for each of us, giving us varying strengths and weaknesses. Methods of mental processing are not easily discernible. Our visible inabilities are always clearer than the underlying mental weaknesses that are causing the problems.

Physical and Mental Processes are Linked

The knowledge that physical and mental processes are linked is not a new concept. For many years, medical researchers have observed how physical coordination problems interfere with the learning process and how physical skills are integrated with mental skills. It is well known that physical and sensory simulation is critical to normal mental growth.

The perceptual skills or processes vital to scholastic learning develop throughout childhood. As a child grows and develops, he or she develops certain strengths and weaknesses in these perceptual processes. In about 20% of the population, under-developed perceptual processes in vital areas needed for learning cause learning difficulties. Learning

Technics has developed a series of neurological/physical exercises that lay a stronger foundation on which the student can build the skills necessary for effective learning. They have done this by creating a series of highly structured and sequential exercises called Physio-Neuro Therapy. These exercises are designed to stimulate and strengthen poorly developed circuits that have made learning difficult. The activities involved in Physio-Neuro Therapy create *"managed overloads"* which strengthen weaknesses in neurological pathways. The managed overloads create a need for juvenile brain cells, which attach themselves to these developing areas of the brain, thereby strengthening areas of weakness by forming new or stronger connections.

$$\binom{6}{}$$

School Studies Confirm Research

In 1989, a school district in Northern Arizona contacted me. This was a small district where the superintendent was also the principal of the high school and would even occasionally substitute as a teacher. Since he was very active in the community, he also interacted with parents and students on social and religious levels. He watched while some of his students struggled both in and out of school. He saw these students continue to struggle with life, just as they had struggled in school, as they grew up, married and had children. Conventional education had not worked for them. He knew there had to be a better way.

Mr. Hart was initially contacted by a mutual friend who knew of the research Learning Technics was doing. Mr. Hart asked if Learning Technics would be interested in setting up a pilot program that would apply this new research to public education. Eager for such an opportunity, I immediately agreed.

At the start of the project, all participants were academically tested using the Stanford Achievement Test and divided into two groups: the control group and the treatment group. Members of the control group continued on in the district's normal intervention programs. The students participating in the treatment group, in the new pilot program which was called "Intercept," were pulled out of class just twenty minutes per day for a one-on-one session with a trained paraprofessional using the Physio-Neuro Therapy Training that Learning Technics had developed. The remainder of the day was spent in the regular classroom environment.

Three months into the project, the superintendent called me. "I would like to revise the pilot program" he said, explaining that the students receiving the benefits of the new Intercept technology had spurted ahead, while the control students all continued to languish. "I can't watch these students continue to struggle just to keep the control group intact. I would like to add them to the group participating in your program." The change was made after deciding that a good indication of program results could still be achieved by comparing the students' SAT scores from the prior year to their scores at the end of the pilot school year.

At the end of the one-year project, all the students were tested again. The entire group had moved up in their ranking, many from nearly the bottom of their class to above average. This improvement was not just significant but highly unusual. The district was delighted and expanded the program the next year.

This expanded program included sixty-one students. All of the students were given SATs. This test ranks students by percentiles from 1 to 100, with the "hundredth percentile" containing the highest ranking students and the "one percentile" the lowest ranking students. This means that a student ranking in the 50th percentile range is an average student. The average percentile score of the students who were beginning the expanded program was 17%. These students were pulled out of class twenty minutes per day, as had been done the previous year, to work with a trained paraprofessional.

When the results of the year-end testing were analyzed, students involved in the expanded Intercept program had improved their class ranking by an average of thirty-three percentile points! In one year, most of the students had moved from struggling students at the bottom of their class to strong, average students.

But a question lingered: Would the changes be permanent? Would percentiles stay the same if no additional assistance was offered or would they decline when help was withdrawn, as is often the case in many intervention programs? The answer came two years later when the students were tested again. This group of students had gained an average of ten more percentile points with no additional help, moving them to the upper third of their class.

The district continued to monitor the therapy students, but in a less formal way. For a number of years after the initial study, the teacher who administered the program for the district compiled a list of the honor roll students from the high school. *On average, twenty percent of the honor roll students came from the neuro-therapy students who were in the bottom 17% of their class in elementary school.* These results were considered remarkable.

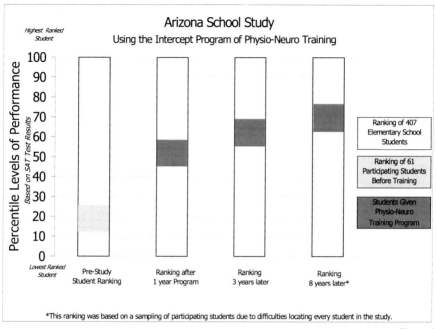

Arizona School Study
Using the Intercept Program of Physio-Neuro Training

Highest Ranked Student

Percentile Levels of Performance
Based on SAT Test Results

100
90
80
70
60
50
40
30
20
10
0

Lowest Ranked Student

Pre-Study Student Ranking

Ranking after 1 year Program

Ranking 3 years later

Ranking 8 years later*

Ranking of 407 Elementary School Students

Ranking of 61 Participating Students Before Training

Students Given Physio-Neuro Training Program

*This ranking was based on a sampling of participating students due to difficulties locating every student in the study.

Figure 6.1

Private School

Armed with statistics from the Arizona study, Learning Technics decided to see what could be done to help more difficult students. We created a private school for children who were at least two years behind in many subjects. These students were taught using standard state approved materials, but Physio-Neuro Therapy Training was added to correct their underlying processing problems.

The students were tested using the Woodcock-Johnson Standard Test For School Achievement before entering the private school and also at the end of each year. The scores considered relevant were: (1) reading (2) spelling (3) math (4) the overall score, or what is called the basic battery. The fifty-one students in the study ranged in age from seven to twelve. Their gain per year prior to enrolling in the school varied widely from subject to subject, but the average composite score showed that, as a group, they had progressed less than six months for every year they had attended school. The poorest progress had been in spelling, which showed almost no growth. This meant these students were falling farther behind their classmates with each passing year. It is understandable that these children often became frustrated and, at times, rebellious because of their inability to succeed in school.

After one year in the private school using Physio-Neuro Therapy Training, the students were again tested. *The average score for the basic battery had increased to one year and four months gain for one year of school, an increase of 146% in performance!*

Test Results

With the unique combination of a solid academic curriculum and Physio-Neuro training, the test results showed these students had experienced a dramatic change in their ability to learn. After returning to a traditional school setting, most of the students were able to maintain grade level without additional special help.

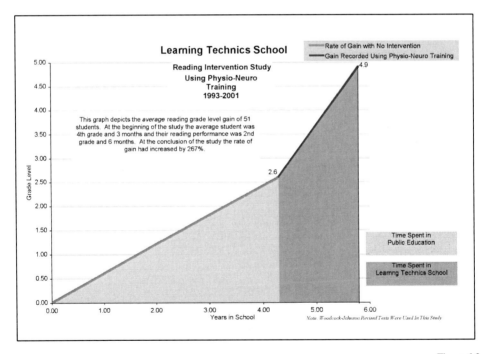

Figure 6.2

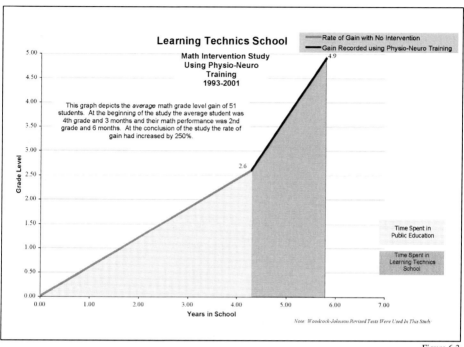

Figure 6.3

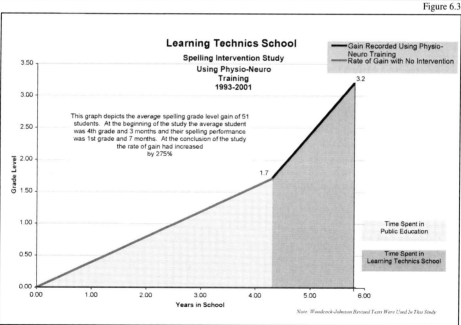

Figure 6.4

Strengthening the Ten Major Neurological Processes Essential to Learning

Although there is a significant number of perceptual processes, Learning Technics has combined these perceptual processes into ten basic groups: *Focus, Cross Patterning, Motor Match, Visual Memory, Tracking, Figure Ground, Directional Discrimination, Position in Space, Size* and *Shape.* The following section contains a brief explanation of each of these processes with a short anecdote demonstrating the symptoms that may be exhibited by an individual lacking in a particular process. Each anecdote is followed by examples of the neurological/physical exercises that are used to strengthen this process. *These exercises constitute only a small portion of the neurological/physical exercises that may be necessary to significantly strengthen a process (or processes) for a struggling individual.* However, it may be very informative for a parent or individual to use these exercises to ascertain whether a particular exercise is difficult for the student, which would indicate that the student could have a problem in that area.

Parents or others who wish to do these exercises with a student should start with the first five or six exercises in the series. This series of five or six exercises should be performed daily until minimum mastery is achieved. A recommended daily practice time is listed following each exercise. When minimum mastery has been achieved, the student should discontinue doing the mastered exercise and begin doing the next exercise in the sequence. Continue doing this until all exercises have been completed. The processes involved in each exercise are listed following the exercise.

1. Focus: The ability to keep the eyes and mind on a specific item or task without loss of concentration

Symptoms:
Difficulty staying on task, poor eye control, poor handwriting

Physical Focus:
Eyes still and converging on a specific focal point

Mental Focus:
Responding to a specific item or task for an appropriate length of time

Students with poor Focus are often labeled Attention Deficit Disorder (ADD). This is a condition in which levels of attention and concentration are inappropriate for the child's age, and the child is often distractible and impulsive. In general, it is the inability to keep the eyes and mind on a task long enough to gather all pertinent information. This inability can have a profound effect on how a student learns. If the eyes and mind cannot Focus long enough to gather all the relevant pieces, the brain must guess at the information and fill in the blanks. This can be one reason a student repeatedly misreads words or misunderstands concepts—because vital parts of needed information are missed. Handwriting can also be affected because the student is unwilling to stay with the task long enough to precisely form and position the letters.

Since this is a diagnosis arrived at by assessing behavior, rather than a medical assessment, there is possibility of error. When a child exhibits the symptoms of ADD, it is assumed there is a chemical imbalance, which is often treated with the use of drugs. For example, if a student is inattentive as the teacher is speaking, the teacher may assume he is ADD. However, the student may be inattentive because he has an auditory processing problem, which makes it difficult for him to interpret what the teacher is saying. (Because he cannot understand what the teacher is saying, his attention goes elsewhere.) By simply observing the student's symptoms, it appears that he is ADD. Doing a complete assessment that can correctly identify the processing problems causing the underlying symptoms can prevent this misdiagnosis. The parent can then use the proper approaches to treat the problem and assist the student in overcoming the difficulties.

Ryan was a bright, impulsive ten-year-old. His mother, Beth, was at her wits' end. He was highly distractible, and always getting into everyone's business to the point of being obnoxious. He was a problem at home, school and at Cub Scouts. Adults and children alike were on edge when he was around. Siblings would often take discipline into their own hands. There were many negative parent/teacher conferences. Ryan was diagnosed ADD and Ritalin was prescribed, but the drug didn't make much difference. The dosage was increased—then increased again. Finally his behavior changed, but little of his personality remained. In the classroom, Ryan was seated some distance from his classmates with a cardboard barrier around his work area preventing him from seeing the other students.

As is usually the case, his symptoms were being addressed. Drugs had deadened any spontaneity and isolation limited distractions. All this was done so he would be easier to manage in the classroom. However, as management became easier, learning diminished. The school seemed relieved at the outcome, but Beth was still fearful for his future.

The cause of all these symptoms/problems was his poorly developed ability to concentrate (Focus). His ability to focus was equivalent to that of a six-year-old, and unless this development was accelerated, nothing would change for Ryan. Through a series of neurological activities conducted over a six-month period, Ryan was able to rejoin his class and gained back his spontaneity. All this was accomplished without Ritalin. An example of the exercises used follows.

Examples of Activities to Improve Focus

Elements of Focus:

1. The eyes must accurately find the object on which to focus
2. The eyes must stop briefly on each point of focus without bypassing or stopping short of the target
3. The eyes must move smoothly from focus point to focus point without stops or hesitations during sweeps
4. The eyes must move with smooth, rhythmic movements

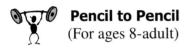

Pencil to Pencil
(For ages 8-adult)

The instructor holds two pencils, with small stickers attached below the eraser, about 12 to 14 inches from the student's face. The pencils are held about 12 inches apart and the stickers should be at the student's eye level. The

Figure 7.1.1

instructor will ask the student to focus on one sticker, then move smoothly to the other. The student will continue moving his or her eyes from sticker to sticker for 10 seconds, with the eyes focusing briefly on each sticker. The instructor watches for any dropping, overshooting, or hesitations of the eyes during the movements and adjusts the speed of the exercise to a slower pace until these difficulties disappear. The student will then practice at this speed until eye movements are smooth and rhythmic. The instructor will gradually increase the speed until the student is able to do the exercise without difficulty at the appropriate speed. If this exercise is difficult, the instructor can hold pencils closer together. As the exercise becomes easier, gradually increase the distance between the pencils to 12 inches.

Materials Needed: Two pencils with stickers attached near the eraser

Practice Time: 3-4 consecutive times per day for 10 seconds until the exercise is easily done

Figure 7.1.2

Minimum Mastery: 22-23 clean, rhythmic movements in 10 seconds for adults (18-19 for students 11 years and under)

Processing Goals:
Focus ~ Can easily track from pencil to pencil with the eyes hesitating briefly on each sticker

*Cross Patterning ~ Can easily track across the vertical midline between the left & right sides of the body

*Tracking ~ Can accurately move eyes from sticker to sticker without dropping the eyes, overshooting the target or hesitations

*Size ~ Can easily move eyes from pencil to pencil with an even rhythm for 10 seconds

*Note: Every activity involves many processes. The starred processes will be introduced later in this section.

 Pencil Direction
(For ages 8-adult)

The instructor holds four pencils, with stickers attached below the eraser, approximately 12 to 14 inches from the student's face. The pencils are held 1 ½ to 2 inches apart with the sticker at the student's eye level. The

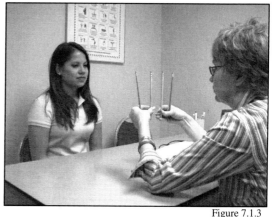
Figure 7.1.3

student will focus his or her eyes on one of the stickers. As the instructor calls out a direction, the student will move his or her eyes to the next pencil in that direction. (If the instructor calls out "left," the student will move the eyes quickly and smoothly to the sticker on the left.) The instructor should change the direction every 2 -3 moves. The instructor will write down the number of clean, consecutive movements done each day and encourage the student to gradually increase the time and number of correct movements. Do this facing in different directions.

Materials Needed: Four pencils with stickers attached near the eraser
Practice Time: 3–4 times per day for 7–8 seconds until the exercise is easily done
Minimum Mastery: Can make 10 clean, correct movements in 7 – 8 seconds (10 seconds for students 9 years and under)

Processing Goals:
Focus ~ Can easily track from pencil to pencil with the eyes hesitating briefly on each sticker
*Tracking ~ Can accurately move eyes from sticker to sticker without dipping, overshooting or hesitations.

*Direction ~ Can easily determine correct direction

*Note: Every activity involves many processes. The starred processes will be introduced later in this section.

> **2. Cross Patterning:** **The ability to coordinate both sides of the body and brain.**

Symptoms:
> Poor comprehension and/or decoding skills;
> difficulty remembering concepts from day to day

Physical Cross Patterning:
> Coordinating movements that cross body midlines
> or use both sides of the body simultaneously

Mental Cross Patterning:
> Cross braining to identify attributes and define
> critical elements

It is well known that the brain is physically divided. An incredibly complex network of nerve fibers called the corpus callosum connects the left and right hemispheres. It is also well known that the two halves of the brain have different functions. The left brain primarily processes language, mathematics, logical thought, etc., while the right brain deals primarily with music, visual impressions, pictures, spatial patterns, etc.

Cross Patterning is the ability of the two sides of the brain to readily share information and cooperate to perform complex tasks. For example, when we read, the left brain is usually responsible for decoding words, while the right brain is responsible for putting these words together into a complete thought or mental picture to help us comprehend what we are reading. If a student has poor Cross Patterning, he may be able to decode the words in the text, but not comprehend the meaning. Or he may have poor decoding skills, but good comprehension. (The left and right hemispheres of his brain are not working effectively together, thus it is difficult for him to both decode the words and comprehend meaning simultaneously.)

It is also common for students with poor Cross Patterning to have poor short-term memory (24 to 36 hours). When a student reviews new information, the storing of this information occurs in different parts of the brain. When he subsequently tries to recall this information, the pieces must be retrieved and reassembled from the various parts of the brain. If Cross Patterning is poor, the various parts of the brain cannot readily merge this information for recall. The result is poor short-term memory.

When doing exercises that involve the simultaneous use of limbs on opposite sides of the body and the crossing of body midlines, we are strengthening the communication between the right and left hemispheres of the brain. As this exchange improves, such skills as short-term memory, comprehension and conceptualization will also improve.

Chris was nine years old and had always found school difficult. He struggled in every subject without exception. Testing was particularly hard on him since it made him painfully aware of his lack of progress. Chris's father, Clint, had taken charge of helping him with homework since his mother had given up in frustration.

Clint was a disciplinarian. He knew that his son was bright, and getting D's and F's was unacceptable. In fact, it was plain foolishness. He knew he could snap him into shape in short order. Chris hadn't passed a spelling test yet this year, so his father thought this was a good place to start. He sat down with Chris at the kitchen table and asked Chris to write each of his twenty spelling words five times. Clint then read the words aloud and had Chris write them as he read them. Chris was then required to write any incorrect words three more times, then write the words out again as his father dictated them. The whole procedure took about forty-five minutes and was grueling for both father and son.

The next night Chris was given the list of twenty words again, and the whole process was repeated. He seemed to have difficulty remembering the words from one night to the next. As the week progressed, Chris became increasingly more exhausted and his mother's stomach churned with anguish for Chris. Clint was confident there would be a passing grade on the next spelling test. On Friday, a dejected

Chris came home with his spelling test. He had received 65%. After all the hard work, the results were the same.

Chris's mother knew he was bright, but she could not understand how he could forget so quickly. She knew something was wrong, but what? His father was still convinced Chris was just not trying. Clint increased the pressure; he knew that a sterner hand would force Chris to improve. However, as the pressure on Chris increased, his performance went down. Their home turned into a pressure cooker of tension, which finally spread to conflicts between Chris's mother and father. Frustrated, Clint often pushed his son to the point of tears.

During spring break the family took a short vacation to visit some friends. When they arrived, their friends' son was marching back and forth across the room spelling words from a chart. "What are you doing?" asked Chris. "I am studying my spelling words," was the response. "Would you like me to spell the words backward?" he asked. "I would just like to be able to spell them forward," murmured Chris. By using the same techniques, Chris could get the grades he hoped for and spell words backward, too.

Examples of Activities to Improve Cross Patterning

Elements of Cross Patterning:

1. The opposite arm and leg should be raised and lowered simultaneously
2. There should be a pause between each step (at least 2 seconds) when both arms and legs are vertical
3. The knee is raised in front of the body with the foot rising slightly behind the body (to mid-calf of the opposite leg)
4. The elbow of the active arm is bent with most of the motion coming from the elbow (both the hand and elbow must cross the vertical midline of the body)
5. The non-active leg remains vertical and the non-active arm slightly behind the vertical midline
6. The number to be spoken is said crisply and precisely when the foot touches the floor (motor match)

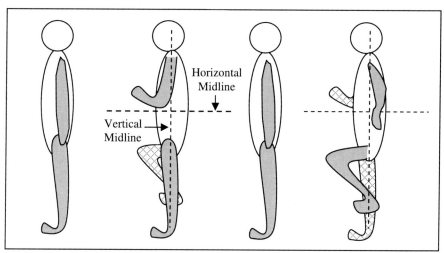

Figure 7.2.1

When doing exercises that involve the simultaneous use of limbs on opposite sides of the body and the crossing of body midlines, we are strengthening the communication between the right and left hemispheres of the brain. All elements of Cross Patterning should be observed while the student marches forward and backward.

Cross Pattern March /Forward and Backward
(For ages 8-adult)

A correct Cross Pattern March contains the following elements: The opposite arm and leg are raised and lowered simultaneously. The knee is raised in front of the body with the foot rising behind the body to mid-calf height. The arm on the opposite side of the body is raised to a horizontal position (with most of the motion coming from the elbow) then lowered to a vertical position to the side. There is a distinct pause of two seconds between each step when the body is still and both hands are at the side. The student will count the steps aloud, saying each number with an exact motor match, which means saying the number at the exact time the foot touches the floor and the arm reaches the vertical position at the side.

When the exercise is easily done and movements are smooth and fluid, add a sticker to the wall at the student's eye level, asking the student to keep his or her eyes steadily focused on the sticker while marching back and forth.

If the above exercise is difficult, ask the student to practice marching in place working on the elements of Cross Patterning (1-6) one step at a time. As each element is mastered, add the next step until a complete cross pattern march is achieved.

Materials Needed: None
Practice Time: 2-3 minutes per day until mastered
Minimum Mastery: Can march both forward and backward with smooth, fluid movements with an exact cross pattern and motor match. Can smoothly coordinate the change from marching forward to marching backward. Can stop 10-12 inches from the wall when marching backward without turning around. Can keep eyes continuously fixed on the sticker while coordinating Cross Pattern March movements.

Forward March

Figure 7.2.2

Backward March

Figure 7.2.3

Processing Goals:
   Focus ~ Can easily keep eyes focused on sticker while marching forward and
      backward
   Cross Patterning ~ Can easily coordinate marching with opposite hand and
      foot and crossing midlines
   *Motor Match ~ Can say the number at the exact time the foot touches the
      floor
   *Position in Space ~ Can judge the position of the body in relationship to the
      wall when marching backward

   Note: Every activity involves many processes. The starred processes will
   be introduced later in this section.

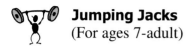 **Jumping Jacks**
(For ages 7-adult)

This exercise is done in the traditional manner, with legs together and hands straight down on the count of "one." The student then jumps while moving legs apart and clapping hands above the head on the count of "two."

Figure 7.2.4

Figure 7.2.5

If the above exercise is difficult, the instructor can ask the student to extend the arms straight out at shoulder height (instead of clapping above the head) while moving the legs apart. The student can also hesitate longer between each move. When these movements are easily done, do the exercise as directed above.

Figure 7.2.6

Figure 7.2.7

Materials Needed: None
Practice Time: 1-2 minutes per day until easily done
Minimum Mastery: Can easily coordinate 15 to 20 jumping jacks while counting (10 jumps for ages 7-8 years)

Processing Goals:
 Cross Patterning ~ Can easily coordinate the movements of hands and feet on opposite sides of the body
*Motor Match ~ Can match the rhythm of the counting with the jumping
*Position in Space ~ Can correlate the relationship of hand movements to movements of the feet

*Note: Every activity involves many processes.   The starred processes will be introduced later in this section.

---

3. Motor Match: The ability of all involved parts of the brain to respond on cue

Symptoms:
   Lack of fluency in physical and mental activities
Physical Motor Match:
   Ability to match physical movements with an auditory cue
Mental Motor Match:
   Ability to respond on cue within an appropriate time frame

A weak Motor Match is often the underlying problem that causes students to struggle with reading fluency. This means that all involved parts of the brain do not coordinate to efficiently process information. When this occurs, the student will read with an extremely choppy or uneven rhythm. The student may also repeatedly misread words. A comparison could be made to an orchestra playing without a conductor. Since a definite tempo has not been established, the whole orchestra may begin to play "out of sync." This is similar to what occurs in the brain if all involved parts do not respond within the needed time frame during the reading process.

Seemingly unrelated symptoms can often be traced back to this mental weakness. Consider the case of eleven-year-old Todd. He was a neat, well-mannered boy who was well liked by his friends and neighbors, but at school he was so clumsy he was considered a klutz.

He disliked sports, but at the same time longed to be involved in the ball games played by his friends at recess and after school. They seemed to have so much fun. He would watch from the sidelines, occasionally throwing a loose ball back to the group. He avoided his coordination problems by withdrawal.

In the classroom Todd shone in math as long as no reading was involved. He could read, but it was a slow and labored process. This was especially true when he was required to read aloud. Both his parents and a private tutor had worked with Todd through the years, but improvement had been agonizingly slow and tedious. Todd's mind would sometimes seem to be processing the words in slow motion. He would even hesitate on smaller words such as "and" and "the"—words he knew. This made his reading extremely choppy and delayed. If Todd was asked to read in front of a group, his difficulties were even more pronounced and embarrassing. His reading comprehension was also affected by his labored, uneven reading, and he would lose his train of thought as he struggled with the words.

It is interesting to note that Todd's jerky reading and poor coordination stemmed from the same problem: his mind's inability to process incoming and outgoing information in a smooth, rhythmic way. Todd addressed his poor coordination problem by withdrawing from sports. His parents addressed his poor reading skills by continual tutoring. Both problems were treated much more successfully by using exercises that improved the efficiency of the neuro-connections in Todd's brain, making it possible for his mind to process information more smoothly and with a predictable rhythm.

Examples of Activities to Improve Motor Match

Elements of Motor Match:

1. The student can match a movement with an auditory activity
2. The student can respond within a given time frame
3. The student can exactly synchronize responses from the various parts of the brain (visual, auditory, speech, kinesthetic, etc.)

Touch, Back, Throw
(For ages 7-adult)

The instructor will demonstrate a series of movements with a Koosh ball (Figure 7.3.4) or beanbag. Each movement is given a name and repeated aloud at the exact time the move is made. (The student will move and name the moves with the instructor.) Examples: "touch" (touch the Koosh to the shoulder); "back" (the hand swings behind the body with the palm facing forward); "throw" (throw the Koosh or beanbag to the student's target hand). The student will repeat these moves with an exact motor match, throwing the Koosh to the instructor. The student will keep the eyes firmly fixed on the instructor's target hand when throwing the Koosh and track the movements of the Koosh with his or her eyes when catching it. (See *focus* and *tracking* in processes below.) The instructor and student will continue practicing the throw and catch movements. When the student can easily do the

Figure 7.3.1

Figure 7.3.2

Figure 7.3.3

exercise using the dominant hand, practice the same movements using the non-dominant hand.

When the above exercise is mastered, one more step is added. After the student does the "touch, back, throw" movements, the student will catch the Koosh saying "catch" at the exact time the Koosh is caught, then switch it to the opposite hand, saying "switch" at the exact time the Koosh is placed in the opposite hand. When this exercise is easily done using the student's dominant hand, it should be done moving in the opposite direction using the non-dominant hand.

Materials Needed: Koosh ball (see figure below) or beanbag

Practice Time: 2-3 minutes per day until the exercise is easily done

Minimum Mastery: The student can keep eyes firmly fixed on the instructor's target hand when throwing and can track the movements of the Koosh ball with the eyes while catching it. The student and trainer can make 8-10 throw/catch movements with both the dominant and non-dominant hand using continuous rhythmic movements without dropping the Koosh ball. (Mastery for ages 7-8 will be 5-6 throw/catch movements.)

Koosh Balls   Figure 7.3.4

Processing Goals:

Focus ~ Can easily keep eyes focused on the instructor's hand when throwing

Cross Patterning ~ Can easily coordinate both sides of the body and cross body midlines

Motor Match ~ Can exactly match saying "touch, back, throw, catch" with corresponding movements

*Tracking ~ Can track all movements of the Koosh when thrown by the instructor and can consistently sequence movement in the correct order

*Note: Every activity involves many processes. The starred processes will be introduced later in this section.

 Double Touch, Back, Throw
(For ages 8-adult)

The following exercise is often too advanced for a younger student and should not be done unless the previous exercise is mastered within 2-3 weeks.

This exercise is done using the same movements as the previous exercise (touch, back, throw, catch, switch), but the student and instructor will use two Koosh balls and will both throw and catch at the same time. The student should start the exercise with the Koosh ball held in the dominant hand. (If the student's dominant hand is the right hand, the instructor will also hold his or her Koosh ball in the right hand.) When movements are smooth and rhythmic, the instructor and student will switch directions (throwing with the opposite hand) using the same movements. When this exercise is mastered, the instructor and student will omit the switch, doing only the "Touch-Back-Throw-Catch" movements. This will be more challenging!

Figure 7.3.5

Figure 7.3.6

Figure 7.3.7

Materials Needed: Two Koosh balls or beanbags
Practice Time: 2-3 minutes per day until the exercise is easily done
Minimum Mastery: The student can keep the eyes firmly fixed on the instructor's target hand when throwing and can track the movements of the Koosh with the eyes when catching. The student can match the exact rhythm of the instructor's movements. The student and instructor can consistently make 8-10 throw/catch movements with both the dominant and non-dominant hand using continuous rhythmic

movements without dropping the Koosh. (Mastery for ages 8-9 will be 5-6 throw/catch movements.)

Processing Goals:
  Focus ~ Can easily keep eyes focused on the instructor's hand when throwing
  Cross Patterning ~ Can coordinate both sides of the body and cross body midlines
  Motor Match ~ Can exactly match saying "touch, back, throw, catch, switch" with corresponding movements
  *Tracking ~ Can track all movements of the Koosh when thrown by the instructor and can consistently sequence movements in the correct order
  *Size ~ Can exactly match the rhythm of instructor's movements

*Note: Every activity involves many processes. The starred processes will be introduced later in this section.

4. Visual Memory: The ability to make mental pictures, form and hold a visual image.

Symptoms:
Poor spelling, decoding, comprehension, poor visual memory

Physical Visual Memory:
The ability to identify and retrieve a visual image previously seen

Mental Visual Memory:
The ability to retrieve visual information previously learned

Visual Memory, or the ability to make mental pictures, is a vital skill in the process of reading. The brain treats each word as a shape. Different combinations of letters create different words or shapes. When reading, the mind must be able to readily recognize all the shapes (words) on a page. It must also put each shape with the correct sound, the word *cat* (KAT) for example, and attach meaning to each shape: four-legged, furry animal.

For most people, it will take five or six exposures to a new shape (word) before our mind will begin to consistently recognize the word. If Visual Memory is weak, however, it may take thirty-five or more exposures before recognition and reading of the new shape becomes fluent. Usually the underlying weakness is not understood, thus the symptom (poor reading) is addressed by having the student read more. Slow improvement does occur, but will not be sustained once the special help stops.

As we read, we must also put words and phrases together to conceptualize the meaning of the words. If we are able to form a clear mental picture or visualize what is taking place in the text, we are easily able to conceptualize meaning. If we are able to visualize the step-by-step procedure as a math concept is being explained, for example, we are easily able to understand and recall the procedure. Visual skills have other important functions as well. They play a major part in helping us recall the correct spelling of words. We must remember what a word looks like (*bouquet* for instance) in order to correctly spell it. This skill can even help people recall where they put their keys. If a student develops the ability to visually retrieve what he has previously seen, he will have a major learning tool at his disposal.

Nick was a boy who suffered from poor visual memory and was several years behind in reading. When Nick and his mother came for an evaluation, a brother and sister accompanied them and sat in the waiting room. After completing the evaluation and discussing the results, the evaluator went with Nick and his mother to the waiting room. There they found his first grade sister reading to her older brother. Nick's shoulders seemed to sag as he said, "Melissa can read and she is only six years old. I can hardly read and I'm ten. I'm so dumb!" Nick's mother responded, "Nick, just because you can't read doesn't mean you're not smart. It just means that Melissa can see a word three or four times and remember it, and you have to see a word fifty times before you remember it." Nick could not understand how he could have a bright mind and still not be able to read. Through a series of neuro-building activities Nick's visual memory improved, his reading increased three grade levels and now Nick reads to his little sister.

Examples of Activities to Improve Visual Memory

Elements of Visual Memory:

1. The student must be able to focus for an adequate study time
2. The student must be able to accurately recognize words and images
3. The student must be able to accurately reproduce words and images
4. The student must be able to accurately recall an image or word for an extended length of time (delayed recall)

 Concentration
(For ages 6-adult)

Using the picture card pairs from an Old Maid deck, turn twelve to twenty cards face down on a table. (Set the "Old Maid" card aside and make sure each card used has a match.) The players will alternate turning two cards at a time face up, trying to locate matching pairs. If a match is not found the player will put the two cards back face down in the same position. If a match is found, the player will keep those cards and take an extra turn. The player that has the most matched cards wins the game.

Materials Needed: Deck of Old Maid cards
Practice Time: (Keep it fun!) 2-3 games per day
Minimum Mastery: Even younger students can develop the ability to remember where matches are located

Processing Goal:
Visual Memory ~ Can recall where matches are located

Basic Shapes in Order
(For ages 6-9)

Cut out 8 or 10 various shapes of different colors then mix them together. The instructor will select 2-3 shapes from the group and arrange them in a row. After the student has looked at the shapes for about 6 to 8 seconds, put the shapes back into the group, mixing them thoroughly with the shapes not used. The student will then look at all the shapes in the group and select the shapes previously used by the instructor and arrange them in the same order. Continue working on this exercise until the student is able to identify four shapes chosen by the trainer and arrange them in the correct order. Once this exercise is easily done, the instructor can use shapes of the same color.

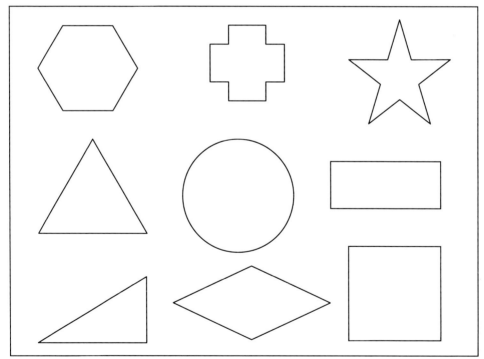

Sample Shapes—enlarge to 200%   Figure 7.4.1

Materials Needed: 9-10 colored shapes cut from card stock
Practice Time: 4-5 times per day until the exercise is easily done.
Minimum Mastery: The student can consistently identify four shapes used by the instructor and arrange them in the correct order.

Processing Goals:
 Visual Memory ~ Can consistently identify 4 shapes used by the instructor
 *Tracking (Sequencing) ~ Can consistently duplicate the correct order of 4 shapes used by the instructor

*Note: Every activity involves many processes. The starred processes will be introduced later in this section.

 Picture Quiz
 (For ages 6-9)

 The following exercise can be used for younger students (ages 6-9) who have poor visual memory.
 The instructor will show the student a simple picture from a book. The student may look at the picture as long as needed. The picture is then taken away and the student is asked 2-3 questions about the picture. The instructor can use questions such as, "What color was the boy's shirt?" or "What did the man have in his hand?" A variety of pictures and questions should be used. If the above exercise is difficult, ask the student to look at the picture and try to remember 3-4 things in the picture to tell the instructor. When this is easily done, do the exercise as directed above.

Materials Needed: Book with simple pictures
Practice Time: 3-4 times per day until the exercise is easily done.
Minimum Mastery: Student can answer 2-3 questions using visual recall from a variety of pictures without assistance.

Processing Goal:
 Visual Memory ~ Can recall 2-3 details from a picture

Focus/Respond Spelling
(For ages 6-adult)

Students can substantially strengthen visual skills by using the following method when studying spelling words:

The instructor will fold a piece of lined paper lengthways and print 3-5 spelling words on consecutive lines using dark ink or a fine marker. The student will say the first word and spell it. (The student must keep his or her eyes firmly fixed on the letters when spelling the word in order to retain a mental picture of the word. If this is difficult, ask the student to point at each letter as the word is spelled.) Turning the page to the blank side, ask the student to visualize the word, in the same position it appears on the opposite side. The student will then spell the word out loud. Again, the student must keep his or her eyes firmly fixed on the blank page in order to accurately visualize the word. If this is difficult, ask the student to point at each letter place on the blank page as the word is spelled. If the student can accurately spell the word, move to the next word. If the student misses the word, repeat the process again, making sure the student points at each letter or letter place as the word is spelled. Repeat this procedure with each word in the group. The instructor will then dictate the words studied that day as the student writes them.

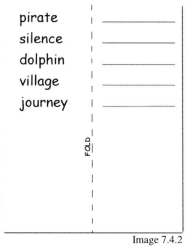

Image 7.4.2

Example of Focus/Respond Spelling Group

The following day, the instructor will dictate the first group as the student writes the words. The student will review any missed words using the Focus/Respond Method explained above. The student will then do the second group of 3-5 words using this method. On the third day, the instructor will dictate groups one and two as the student writes them. The student will then study the third group using the Focus/Respond Method. Continue using this method until all spelling words can be accurately written.

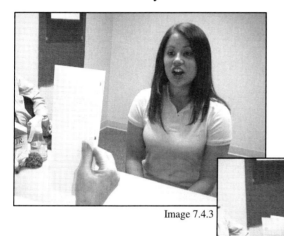

Image 7.4.3

Image 7.4.4

The instructor should observe the student's eyes, making sure that the eyes stop on each letter or letter place as the name is said. Remind the student to spell the word slowly while using visual memory to form a mental picture.

If longer words are difficult, the instructor may divide the words into visual chunks for easier recall. Visual chunks are often smaller than syllables. (See examples below.)

sis ter	**but ter fly**	**co co nut**
to get her*	**fat her***	**an i mal**

| **per son** | **ele ph ant*** | **gi ant** |
| **ham mer** | **sp lin ter*** | **pen cil** |

*Examples of words that are easier to visualize when not grouped in syllables.

Materials Needed: Lined paper and pen or fine marker
Practice Time: Do 3-5 words daily
Minimum Mastery: The student can accurately visualize spelling words and can recall the correct spelling of the words the next day.

Processing Goals:
  Focus ~ Keeping eyes on the letter or letter place until each letter is named and keeping eyes on each word until completed.
  Visual Memory ~ Can accurately visualize each word on the blank page and can accurately recall correct spelling in daily reviews
 *Tracking ~ The eyes can track smoothly from letter place to letter place. The student can visualize letters in the correct order.

*Note: Every activity involves many processes. The starred processes will be introduced later in this section.

---

5. Tracking: **The ability to move the eyes from focal point to focal point with smooth, accurate movements. The ability to respond in the correct sequence.**

Symptoms:
       Difficulty with fluency, skipping words or lines
Physical Tracking:
       Eyes moving smoothly from focal point to
       focal point with smooth, accurate movements
Mental Tracking:
       Responding in the correct sequence

   One of the major visual skills needed to perform the act of reading is the ability of the eyes to track. During the act of reading, the eyes must accurately follow the lines of the text and move precisely from one word to the next. It is a surprising fact that some students do not naturally develop this critical skill. In one study (Koslowe 1995), "Visual tracking was found to be the major visual deficit in a group of 100 elementary school children referred to a center for reading disabilities."

The young reader must learn to briefly focus on each word then move smoothly to the next while accurately reading the lines of the text. If the student has not developed this skill, he may constantly lose his place and/or skip lines or words. Poor Tracking can even cause the student to reverse words such as *"saw"* and *"was"* or *"on"* and *"no."* (The eyes, in moving to the next word, may slightly overshoot and in the act of moving back will inadvertently see the word backward.) A student who struggles with eye Tracking will often use his finger while reading to assist the eyes in tracking the text.

Joe was a nine-year-old who struggled with reading and was two years behind. His father worked as an executive for a public utility company and his mother worked part time as a volunteer in a public school. Both were college graduates. Joe's sisters, who were four and six years older respectively, were good students and loved sports, especially baseball. They had been trying to teach Joe how to play baseball for years, with little success. In frustration, one sister said, "He is never going to be able to catch a ball. When it comes toward him he closes his eyes and hopes the ball hits his mitt. When batting, he either swings at everything or swings at nothing. Either way, he never hits the ball." He wanted so much to be like his sisters, good in school and baseball. Now, after years of trying, expectations were dwindling.

I was on a business trip to the city in which the family lived. I was asked by Joe's father to evaluate Joe. I didn't have a complete assessment package, but did what I could. As his father watched, Joe was asked to visually track an object that I moved in various patterns. Joe's eyes jerked as they tried to stay on the object. Even when it was static, he had trouble focusing on it. His father watched in amazement.

That night at home, with his mother and sisters watching, Joe's father went through some of the same maneuvers with the same outcome. As his sisters watched, one suddenly blurted out, "No wonder he can't catch a ball. He can't find it." His father thought, "Yes, and now I know why he can't read."

Joe's difficulties with reading and baseball were obvious to his family, but the fact that his mind could not aim his eyes was a startling revelation. Now they understood why the hours of academic tutoring and baseball practice hadn't made a difference.

Examples of Activities to Improve Tracking

Elements of Tracking:

1. The student can smoothly track a moving object
2. The student can accurately track from focal point to focal point
3. The student can reproduce a visual, auditory or kinesthetic sequence

Ball Tracking with Stress
(For ages 8-adult)

The student is instructed to lie on the floor. A small rubber ball, suspended on a string, is hung about 16-18 inches above the bridge of the student's nose (Figure 7.5.1). The student is asked to follow the ball with his eyes as the instructor puts the ball in motion, moving it for an equal amount of time in vertical, horizontal, diagonal, or circular motions (see Figure 7.5.4 on page 58). The instructor can start by doing each direction 20 seconds then gradually increase the time in 5-second increments for each direction. The instructor should keep the ball within the student's field of vision (approximately 18" from dead center). When this exercise is easily done, the instructor will add stress (distractions) in the form of questions or conversation.

It is essential that the body remain relaxed and quiet during the entire exercise. The kinesthetic or ADD student will often want to keep the body in constant motion, especially while talking or taking in information (listening). This is a distinct disadvantage in a classroom environment, as it will prevent the student from focusing on the task at hand, whether it be listening to the teacher or doing seatwork.

If the above exercise is difficult, the instructor can ask the student to count each swing of the ball (this creates a sensory cross check). A good goal would be ten swings in each direction, with the eyes remaining continuously fixed on the ball. The instructor can further simplify the exercise by asking the student to point at the ball as it swings.

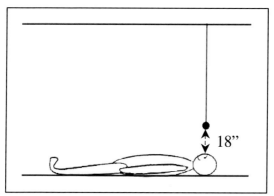

Figure 7.5.1

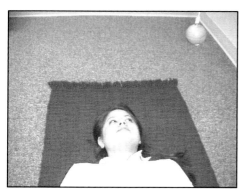

Figure 7.5.2

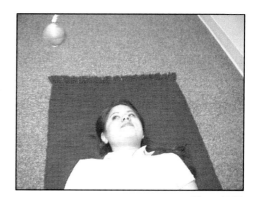

Figure 7.5.3

NOTE: Some symptoms of eyestrain are red or watery eyes, headache or continual blinking.   If the student begins to exhibit any of these symptoms, <u>do not increase tracking time for 5-7 days</u>. After 5-7 days the instructor may begin to increase tracking time as per instructions above.   If student's eyes are light sensitive, the instructor may want to utilize natural lighting.

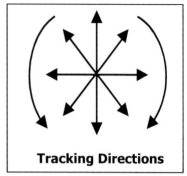

Tracking Directions

Figure 7.5.4

Materials Needed: 8-10 ft of heavy cord attached to a small rubber ball (see figure 7.5.5) suspended from the ceiling

Practice Time: Work up to tracking one minute per year of age while carrying on a conversation or answering questions. (Maximum time for adults - 15 minutes)

Minimum Mastery: Can keep eyes continuously fixed on the ball as it moves without eyestrain or extra movements. (The eyes are to stay continuously on the ball during the entire time span of the tracking exercise.)

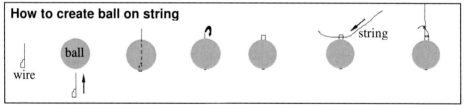

How to create ball on string

wire   ball   string

Figure 7.5.5

Processing Goals:

Focus ~ Can keep eyes continuously fixed on moving ball, tracking for 1 minute per year of age (15 minutes max. for ages 16-adult)

Cross Patterning ~ Eyes can track across vertical midline

Tracking ~ Eyes can track movements of the ball

*Figure Ground ~ The eyes and mind can stay focused during the distraction of stress

*Note: Every activity involves many processes. The starred processes will be introduced later in this section.

Sentence Repeat
(For ages 8-adult)

Using material at the student's reading level, the instructor slowly reads a sentence or partial sentence (8-10 words). The instructor will say the words clearly at about two words per second. (Longer hesitations will increase the difficulty of the exercise.) The student will echo back the sentence, slowly repeating the exact words in the same order.

If the above exercise is difficult, the instructor can read fewer words. For example, start the exercise using five words. When the student can successfully repeat five words, move to six words, etc. Continue the exercise, gradually increasing the amount of words read until the student is successfully repeating 8-10 words. The instructor can further simplify the exercise by using words that make a complete thought.

Materials Needed: Book at appropriate reading level
Practice Time: 6-8 times per day until easily done
Minimum Mastery: Can consistently and accurately repeat 8-10 words read by the instructor

Processing Goals:
Focus ~ Can keep mind on the task long enough to repeat exact information given by the instructor
Tracking ~ Can accurately repeat words in the correct sequence

Digit Repeat
(For ages 8-adult)

Using the number list (Figure 7.5.5), the instructor will read a series of numbers in a monotone voice with a short, equal pause between each digit. The student will then repeat the numbers in the correct sequence. The instructor will start with the number of digits that is age appropriate for the student. (The instructor may test the student with 4 digits. If this is easily done, move to five digits. If it is difficult, move back to three digits.)

The instructor will read 4 digits with a short ½ second pause between each digit. The student will then repeat the four numbers in the correct sequence. When the student is able to consistently repeat four numbers in the correct sequence, the instructor will do the exercise using 5 digits. The instructor will continue to increase the number of digits until the student is able to accurately repeat the appropriate number for his/her age level. (See Minimum Mastery.)

If the student is ready to move from four digits to five digits, but has extreme difficulty when an additional digit is added, the instructor can use the following steps: The instructor will give the student four digits. The student will repeat the four digits. The instructor will then give an additional digit (only one). The student will repeat the four digits previously given, plus the single digit given last by the instructor. When this exercise is easily done, revert to the initial exercise above using 5 digits. Continue using this method until mastery is reached for the appropriate age level.

The following number groups can be varied by doing groups forward, then backward or giving the last four digits in a sequence then the first three.

9-4-2-7-8-3-5	9-8-3-6-0-4-1	7-5-3-0-1-4-8
5-2-9-4-6-0-8	5-8-1-9-3-7-0	1-9-2-6-4-8-3
4-9-3-7-8-2-6	3-6-2-7-9-4-1	2-4-7-9-6-0-1
2-7-1-8-4-9-0	6-8-4-0-2-5-3	8-5-4-1-6-3-7
6-3-5-2-8-4-7	9-4-2-1-7-3-6	6-3-5-7-1-9-2

Figure 7.5.5

Materials Needed: None
Practice Time: 6–8 number sequences per day until mastered

Minimum Mastery: Can consistently repeat a correct sequence of numbers for the appropriate age level. (Appropriate mastery for ages 7-8 is 5 digits; 9-11 is 6 digits; 12-adult is 7 digits.)

Processing Goals:
  Focus ~ Can keep the mind focused on the task long enough to accurately repeat a series of digits
  Tracking ~ Can repeat a series of digits in the correct sequence

6. Figure Ground: The ability to focus on a specific item or task amid distraction.

Symptoms:
  Easily distracted, responds to all stimuli within the surrounding environment
Physical Figure Ground:
  Ability to focus on a physical focal point against a competing background
Mental Figure Ground:
  Ability to stay focused on a specific task amid distraction.

The volume of stimuli coming to the brain at any given time is incredible. The brain must rapidly sort the pertinent incoming information from the insignificant. (If a student in a classroom is responding appropriately, he will ignore the person tapping a pencil in the next seat or the noise in the hall and focus on the important information being given by the teacher.) If the sorting of information does not properly occur, the brain is bombarded with an overabundance of stimuli and the student tends to respond inappropriately or may display inappropriate behavior.

The process of Figure Ground is the ability to focus on the "figure" or the important stimuli (the teacher's instruction) against a background of competing stimuli (the tapping of the pencil or the noise in the hall). Developing the process of Figure Ground is vital for a student that exhibits the symptoms of ADD. By developing his or her ability to focus on the most important task at hand (while ignoring distractions), the student soon learns to respond to significant stimuli and ignore the unimportant.

Abbie found elementary school easy at first. But as the material in each grade became more diverse, she had to do more work on her own. School became harder. This trend continued year after year. She addressed this increased difficulty by working harder and trying to remember *everything*. If she did this, she was sure she would get a good grade on her tests.

As a second semester freshman in college Abbie felt incapable of going any farther. She conceded to a friend that, when she read a textbook or listened to a lecture, she couldn't tell which facts were important and which was background material. "I never know what is going to be on the exam. It all seems to be important," she said. "I can't figure out what the professor thinks is important and remember it for his tests. It's a huge guessing game and I'm losing."

At the beginning of Abbie's second semester, she went to the bookstore to purchase the books that were required. One of the books was a used book. The past owner of the book had highlighted numerous passages. She paid no attention to these markings and studied in her usual way. As was her custom, when she got her tests back she would find the answers to the questions missed in her textbook. As she went through her exams using the book, she was amazed that almost all the answers to the exam questions were highlighted. She thought to herself, "The person that had this book before must have been a very good student. I could be a good student, too, if I knew what was going to be on the exam." The problem was that Abbie had poorly developed figure ground, the neurological process of finding what she should focus on in a background of other peripheral information.

Examples of Activities to Improve Figure Ground

Elements of Figure Ground:

1. The student can focus amid distraction
2. The student can identify the "figure" (main point of focus) within a background distraction
3. The student can process the "figure" (main point of focus) while being aware of the background (distraction)

 Draw and Sing
(For ages 7-adult)

The instructor will ask the student to draw simple pictures while counting or singing the ABC's or other songs. An older student can write his/her name or other familiar words while singing.

Materials Needed: Whiteboard and marker or paper and pencil
Practice Time: 4 – 6 pictures or words per day
Minimum Mastery: Can easily draw pictures or spell simple words while singing

Processing Goal:
Figure Ground ~ Can draw or spell simple words while singing

 Peripheral Letter Focus
(For ages 7-9)

The following exercise can be done using a dry erase marker and board. (A vinyl sheet protector with a piece of 8½ x 11 white card stock placed inside can also be used as a board.) The dry erase board (or page) should be placed on a wall at the student's eye level. The instructor will place a half-inch dot near the center of the board. The instructor will then draw eight letters, approximately ¾ inch in size, around the dot. Letters should be positioned about 2 inches from the dot. (See Figure 7.6.1) The instructor should not use letters that are visually similar in the circle, such as "Q" and "O" or "E" and "F".

With the student positioned 16–18 inches from the chart, the instructor will ask the student to look at the dot. While the student's eyes are on the dot, the instructor will name one of the letters around the dot. While keeping the eyes continuously on the dot, the student will place his finger on the correct letter. If the student is able to keep his eyes on the dot while pointing at the letter, the instructor will erase that letter. If his eyes move, the student will try again using another letter. The student can challenge himself to clear the board in 8-10 tries.

If the above exercise is difficult, the instructor can use fewer letters that are placed closer to the central dot. Once the exercise is easily done, move to the next exercise.

Materials Needed: Dry-erase marker and board (or vinyl sheet protector with 8 ½ x 11 card stock placed inside)
Practice Time: 2-3 circles of letters per day until mastered
Minimum Mastery: Can keep eyes continuously on the dot while pointing at all eight letters in the circle

Processing Goals:
  Focus ~ Can keep eyes continuously focused on the dot while pointing at each letter
  Figure Ground ~ Can isolate the appropriate letter

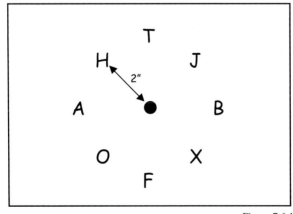

Figure 7.6.1

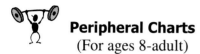

Peripheral Charts
(For ages 8-adult)

The instructor will hang one of the peripheral charts (see Figures 7.6.2, 7.6.3, and 7.6.4) with the third horizontal line of letters at the student's eye level. With the student positioned 16-18 inches directly in front of the chart, he or she is instructed to look at the "O" in the center line. The instructor will name a letter and the student will locate the letter as it is named using his peripheral vision with the eyes remaining steadily fixed on the "O". He will signal the instructor that he has found the letter by placing his pointer finger on it. (The student's eyes are to remain firmly fixed on the "O" during the entire process.) The instructor will continue naming letters as the student points to the letters named. The instructor may start with letters immediately surrounding the "O" and move outward as peripheral skill increases.

Continue working on the exercise until the student has done 8–10 letters. **<u>NOTE: The trainer will use a different chart each day and vary the letters located to prevent memorization of the charts. Charts should be enlarged to 190% before using.</u>**

Materials Needed: Three peripheral letter charts
Practice Time: 8–10 letters per day using one chart
Minimum Mastery: Can keep eyes firmly fixed on the "O" while finding letters with peripheral vision.

Processing Goals:
 Focus ~ Can keep eyes firmly fixed on the "O" during the entire exercise
 Figure Ground ~ Can keep eyes on the letter "O" while being distracted by
   locating letter in periphery

Peripheral Letter Charts

P S Y

M J G F W

T Z R O B K D

U L A N V

Q H X

Figure 7.6.2

C B R

Q L A K M

D S X O J U V

F W G H P

Z T Y

Figure 7.6.3

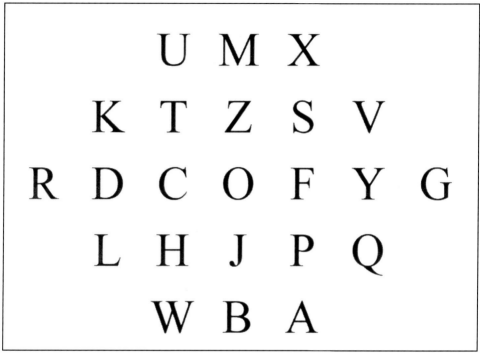

Figure 7.6.4

Enlarge charts 190% before using

7. Directional Discrimination: The ability to distinguish directional orientation without relying on visual clues.

Symptoms:
Letter or word reversals, problems identifying left and right, difficulty with a sequence of instructions

Physical Directional Discrimination:
Ability to identify correct physical orientation such as left, right, up, down, etc.

Mental Directional Discrimination:
Using correct orientation in activities such as reading & writing (differentiating between "d" and "b" , "on" and "no" or "saw" and "was")

As young children, our intake of knowledge depends on our ability to identify objects in spite of where or how they are seen (upside down, backward or in a book). Even a young child can identify a chair whatever the design, size, shape or where it is located. However, when the child starts school, there is a significant jump in the level of visual and Directional Discrimination needed. He must differentiate between characters that look very similar such as *d*'s & *b*'s and *p*'s & *q*'s and between words such as *mom* and *wow* and *on* and *no*. Reversals are normal for younger students, but if these problems continue after the second grade, there is a good chance the student is experiencing problems with directionality. (Reversals can be caused by problems other than poor directionality—see tracking.)

Poor directionality can be devastating for a student. It can make reading laborious, spelling almost impossible and writing frustrating. Directional processing problems start with poor body awareness. (The student must first understand what is up, down, left and right in relationship to the body.) Asking the student to do activities in which he or she must instantaneously determine directional orientation and respond to it can reinforce these skills.

The following example gives us some understanding of why students struggling with directionality have difficulty with reading, writing and spelling. They may mentally process the following sentence; "Dealing with poor directionality can be devastating for a student" as, "Daeling with boor birtionaltiy can de bevastating for a stubent." Sometimes a person with directional processing problems is called dyslexic.

Carl was at the bottom of his sixth grade class. He had attended Washington Elementary School since the second grade and his difficulties were well known to the faculty. He was a poor reader and speller. He had a hard time understanding verbal instructions. Carl reversed "b's" and "d's" and frequently got letters and numbers out of sequence. In earlier years he had worked hard at his school assignments, but over time he had become complacent. His work ethic and self-esteem had deteriorated. He had turned into the class clown. This way no one knew that he couldn't perform academically. They thought he was just joking around.

Finally, all these problems were traced back to one mental processing weakness called sequencing or direction. This is the mental process we all use to put pieces of information together in the correct order. Once this diagnosis was made, his teachers wondered why they hadn't recognized this common thread through all his difficulties. In hindsight, it was so clear.

Carl was enrolled in the Learning Technics Intercept Program at school that addressed this problem and slowly the symptoms began to fade. He was no longer the struggling class clown the school staff knew.

Examples of Activities to Improve Directional Discrimination

Elements of Directional Discrimination:

1. The student can determine left and right in relationship to the body
2. The student can determine correct directionality

 Hands Across the Body
(For ages 6-10)

The instructor calls out a part of the body and a direction such as "left elbow." The student will respond by quickly touching the left elbow with the right hand. (The body part should be touched with the hand on the opposite side of the body.) <u>The instructor should change the direction in which the student is facing 2-3 times during the daily exercise. This will strengthen directional orientation, which is based on the body rather than the surrounding environment.</u>

If this exercise is difficult, do the exercise without the directional component until all body parts are learned, then add a directional command with the body part. **Note:** Children seven years old should know most body parts. Children nine years and above should know all body parts.

Materials Needed: None

Practice Time: Name 6-8 body parts per day until the exercise is easily done.

Minimum Mastery: The student should be able to respond quickly (within 1–2 seconds) with the correct body part using the hand on the opposite side of the body.

Processing Goals:
  Cross Patterning ~ Can easily coordinate movements that cross body midlines and use both sides of the body
  Direction ~ Can accurately determine left from right

 Left/Right Action Chart
  (For ages 8-adult)

The Left/Right Action Chart (Figure 7.7.2) will be placed on the wall at the student's eye level. Standing 4-5 feet from the wall, facing the chart, the student will move from left to right through the chart responding to each action or command in approximately 2 seconds. Each time the student does the exercise, the instructor will pick a different direction for him/her to move through the chart. Vary the direction by doing the chart forward, backward and zigzag. The student should respond to each command with smooth, rhythmic body movements <u>without verbalizing the commands</u>. (The actions are coded by using the first letter of the following words: **L**eft, **R**ight, **H**and, **F**oot, **U**p, **B**ack, **S**ide, and **W**ave. Figure 7.7.1.)

To prevent the student from using the room for directional orientation, the instructor should change the direction in which the student is facing each time the chart is done. This will strengthen directional orientation that is based on the body, not the environment surrounding the student.

If the above exercise is difficult, the student can do the exercise saying each command out loud. When this is easily done, do the exercise as directed above.

Materials Needed: Left/Right Action Chart

Practice Time: 3-4 times per day until the exercise is easily done.

Minimum Mastery: Can respond accurately to each command with a smooth, even rhythm. Can move through entire chart within 25-30 seconds without stops or hesitations. Can accurately respond to commands when chart is moved from wall to wall.

Examples of Actions

Figure 7.7.1

Processing Goals:
    Focus ~ Can easily keep mind on the task and eyes on the page long enough to make correct responses.
    Tracking ~ Can respond in the correct sequence
    Direction ~ Can respond with the correct direction and side of the body

Left/ Right Action Chart

LHW	RFB	LHS	LFU
RFU	LHB	RFS	RHW
LFS	RHS	LFB	RHB

Figure 7.7.2

Enlarge 150% before using

 **Drill Sergeant with Stress**
(For ages 9-adult)

The student will march in a cross pattern, turning 45 degrees as the instructor calls out a direction. The student will respond when he/she is ready by turning in the direction called out and saying the direction as the foot on that side of the body touches the floor. The instructor should change the direction every 3-5 steps.

Practice Time: 2-3 minutes per day until exercise is easily done
Minimum Mastery: Can accurately respond within 3 seconds by turning the right direction and using the correct foot 10 consecutive times while marching in a cross pattern

Processing Goals:
Cross Patterning ~ Can coordinate opposite hand and foot
Motor Match ~ Can give an auditory response at the exact time the foot touches the floor
Direction ~ Can respond by turning in the correct direction and using the correct foot

8. Position in Space: The ability to determine relationships.

Symptoms:
Difficulty with coordination and social skills; easily lost or disoriented in unfamiliar settings

Physical Position in Space:
Ability to identify where they are in relationship to their environment and to determine where objects are in relationship to their surroundings

Mental Position in Space:
Ability to determine relationships within a given concept

Some people are very shy and others are obnoxious. Some even bounce between the two. Understanding how to relate to others is a function of Position in Space. It is also involved in knowing where your body is in relationship to its surroundings or knowing where your car is on the highway as you are driving. It plays a part in knowing how things relate to each other within a given environment or fit into the "big picture." Being able to organize material such as an outline or study guide is difficult if you do not understand how the concepts relate to each other or to what you already know.

Devin's slow development of the neurological process of position in space began to surface in the second grade. He had trouble understanding such concepts as personal ownership and "I had it first." He also tried to dominate most activities involving other children. Consequently he had many arguments with his classmates and with adults who tried to mediate the difficulties. Friendships were short with only a few playmates able to tolerate Devin for very long. He felt lonesome and picked on.

As the years passed, things didn't improve very much. The situations changed with age; however, conflicts were still numerous. Now instead of feeling picked on, he felt misunderstood. Devin's teenage years were particularly painful as friends became more and more important. Friends would come and go as most could not tolerate his intrusive, obnoxious behavior. High school was a terrible place, not because he was a poor student but, rather, because of his social skills. Most students steered clear of Devin.

Today at thirty, he is still struggling with the same position in space problem that plagued him in elementary school. He has graduated from college and has only a few friends—mostly younger. He has dated many females, but only for short periods of time. Steady employment has been hard to maintain because of his difficulty getting along with his employer and fellow workers.

Examples of Activities to Improve Position in Space

Elements of Position in Space:

1. The student can determine the position of his or her body in relationship to other objects
2. The student can determine the position of objects in relationship to their surrounding environment
3. The student can determine the relationship of ideas within a given concept

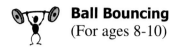 **Ball Bouncing**
(For ages 8-10)

The student is shown how to bounce a large ball using one hand at a time. When this exercise is easily done, the student will dribble the ball while alternating hands (one bounce per hand). The student should be able to smoothly change hands while bouncing the ball with an even rhythm.

If this exercise is difficult, the instructor can simplify the exercise by asking the student to use both hands to dribble the ball. Another simplification could be bouncing the ball 2-3 times with each hand. When these simplifications are easily done, do the exercise as instructed above.

Materials Needed: A large ball that will easily bounce such as a Four-Square Ball
Practice Time: 3-4 minutes per day
Minimum Mastery: Can consistently bounce the ball 8-10 times while alternating hands with minimum body movement

Processing Goals:
   Tracking ~ The eyes can track movements of the ball
   Position in Space ~ Can dribble the ball with good body control and timing
      while alternating hands

 Scarf Juggling Basic
(For ages 7-adult)

The student will start with a scarf in each hand. The upper arms are held loosely at the side of the body with the lower arms extending forward, perpendicular to the body. The student will throw the first scarf with the dominant hand, throwing across the body and slightly above the head on the opposite side while saying, "throw". The student will then throw the second scarf across the body and above the head on the opposite side of the body while saying, "throw." He or she will then bring the hands back to the original position, catching the first scarf as it comes down, then catching the second scarf with the other hand. The student will say "catch" with an exact motor match as each scarf is caught. (The right hand will catch the scarf thrown by the left hand and the left hand will catch the scarf thrown by the right hand. Figure 7.8.1.) The student will practice throwing and catching until he or she is able to do several rotations with smooth, even movements.

If the above exercise is difficult, the instructor can ask the student to practice throwing the scarves without catching them. When this is easily done, do the exercise as directed above.

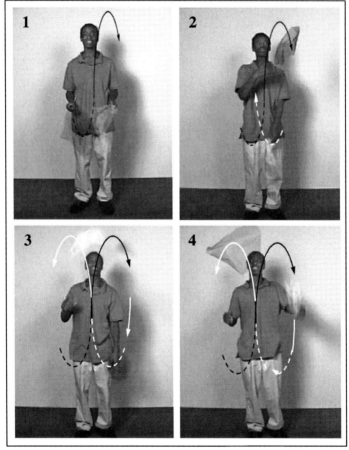

Figure 7.8.1

Materials Needed: 2 small light-weight juggling scarves. They can be made using two 12"x 12" squares of tulle from your local fabric store.
Practice Time: 3-4 minutes per day until easily done
Minimum Mastery: The student can juggle two scarves 10-12 times without stops, hesitations, or movements of the feet while using smooth, rhythmic movements.

Processing Goals:

Cross Patterning ~ Can coordinate hands and cross body midline to juggle scarves

Motor Match ~ Can say "throw" and "catch" at the exact time the scarves are thrown and caught

Tracking ~ Can sequence throwing and catching scarves in the correct order

Position in Space ~ Can judge where scarves are in relationship to hands and body

 **Beanbag Juggling**
(For ages 9-adult)

The student will stand with his or her feet about 12–14 inches apart. The student's upper arms should be held loosely at the side with lower arms and hands extending out horizontally in front of the body (palms up). The student will hold a beanbag in both the dominant and non-dominant hand. The student will throw the beanbag in the dominant hand, angling the throw slightly toward the opposite side of the body. (If thrown properly, the beanbag will come to the apex of the throw approximately 8–10 inches above the head on the opposite side of the body.) The student will immediately throw the beanbag in the non-dominant hand in the same manner. (Both beanbags will be in the air at the same time.) As the first beanbag comes down, the student will move the non-dominant hand into position to catch the beanbag and immediately throw it again to the opposite side of the body. The student will immediately catch the second beanbag with the dominant hand and repeat the same movements. The student will continue throwing and catching in this manner saying "throw-throw" as the beanbags are thrown and "catch-catch" as the beanbags are caught (Figure 7.8.2).

Materials Needed: 2 beanbags
Practice Time: 2 -3 minutes per day until easily done
Minimum Mastery: The student can throw beanbags with an exact motor match, saying, "throw-throw" when throwing and "catch-catch" while catching. The student can consistently make 8–10 "throw-throw,

catch-catch" movements without dropping the beanbags. (Mastery for ages 9–10 will be 5–6 consecutive throws.)

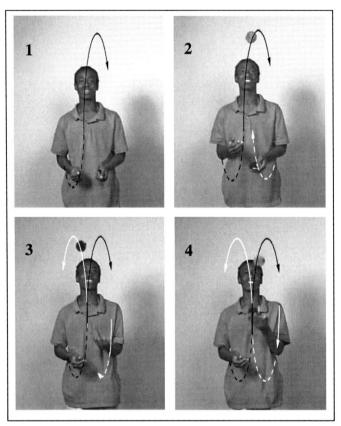

Figure 7.8.2

Processing Goals:
Cross Patterning ~ Can simultaneously coordinate hand and arm movements on both sides of the body

Motor Match ~ Can say "throw" and "catch" at the exact time the beanbags are thrown and caught

Position in Space ~ Can consistently throw beanbags to the same position relative to the body when coordinating throws. Can correctly position hands to catch beanbags.

*Size ~ Can throw the beanbags with consistent magnitude. Can throw and catch beanbags with a consistent rhythm

*Note: Every activity involves many processes. The starred processes will be introduced later in this section.

9. Size: The ability to determine importance or magnitude.

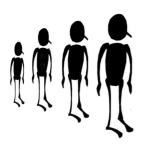

Symptoms:
> Poor sense of timing; difficulty with the time component of task management; misinterpretation of the importance of situations (can underreact or overreact). The inability to judge physical size

Physical Size:
> Understanding magnitude

Mental Size:
> Ability to determine relative importance

All information coming to the brain has an element of magnitude or Size. When a task must be completed within a certain time frame, we must accurately judge the Size of the task and the time frame it will take to complete the task. Some of the common symptoms of inadequate processing of Size are the inability to organize tasks in a timely manner (misjudging the time it will take to do a homework assignment, thus running out of time) and/or being chronically late for engagements and deadlines. Overreacting to an event also involves the judgment of Size. (The person may attach greater meaning to an insignificant event or may underreact to a significant event.)

James was a bright, inventive, nine-year-old. He lived in a neighborhood with four other boys about his age. He would often lead the other boys on scavenger hunts to a nearby dump; then they would haul their treasures to the top of a juniper-covered hill nearby. There they would build forts and spend many long, enjoyable hours on these projects. There were no drawings, specifications, or completion schedules. James only had to use his great creativity for these projects. He spent every spare moment on the hill and organizing his friends to complete his projects.

School was different. School was structured with required completion times for homework and other assignments. The teacher determined what was to be done, how it was to be done, and when it was to be completed. The teacher required the students to work independently on projects and assignments. When James completed one assignment, he was to go to his file and start the next assignment. He was responsible for organizing himself in such a way that, at the end of the week, he had completed all the work in the file. In this environment, he was forced to establish how long each assignment would take to complete and how many pages he would be required to do each day in order to finish all the assignments by the end of the week. He had great difficulty planning and completing his work on time. To all observers James was highly unorganized but the truth was he could not tell the size of a task, how long it was going to take to complete, and when he should start in order to complete it on time.

Examples of Activities to Improve Size

Elements of Size:

1. The student can successfully handle the time component of task management
2. The student can make an appropriate response to events (determine appropriate magnitude to attach to events)
3. The student can make accurate judgment of physical size
4. The student is aware of correct timing and/or rhythm

 Copy the Letter Size
(For ages 8-adult)

Using words of 4 to 6 letters at the appropriate grade level, the instructor will print the words (in lower case letters) on lined paper. The student will then print the words in lower case letters, copying the size of the instructor's letters. The letters in each word should be uniform in size, evenly spaced and sitting on the line. (Tall letters, such as "t's" and "l's", should be about twice the height of small letters.) Letters should be formed from <u>top to bottom</u> using a consistent pattern. The instructor will vary the letter sizing in each word written. (See Figure 7.9.1)

Materials Needed: "Copy the Letter Size" form (Figure 7.9.2)
Practice Time: Do 4-6 words per day until the exercise is easily done
Minimum Mastery: The student can copy the size of the instructor's letters and form a series of letters that are uniform in size, evenly spaced and sitting on the linen.

Processing Goals:
  Position in Space ~ Can form a series of letters that are evenly spaced and sitting on the line
  Size ~ Can accurately reproduce the size of the instructor's letters

Example of Copy Letter Size

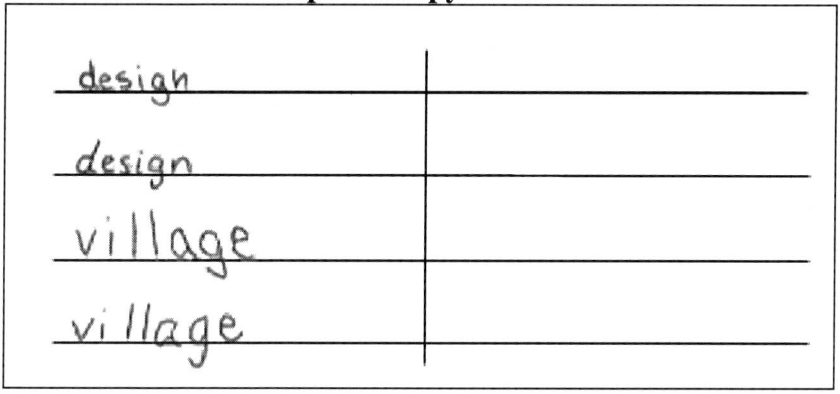

Figure 7.9.1

Copy the Letter Size

Figure 7.9.2

Enlarge to 150% before using

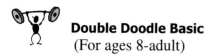

Double Doodle Basic
(For ages 8-adult)

Using two dry erase markers and a whiteboard, the student will draw circles, squares, triangles, etc., using both hands. The non-dominant hand will draw in a mirror image of the dominant hand. It doesn't matter where you start the figure you are drawing, but the non-dominant hand must mirror the movements of the dominant hand.

For example, if the student is drawing a triangle (starting at the top), the first movement of both hands would be moving downward and away from center. The second movement would be from the outside toward the center. The third movement would be slanted away from the center to the original starting place (see Figures 7.9.3 and 7.9.4). The student should hold the marker in the dominant and non-dominant hands the same way (with three fingers as shown). The student can determine the size of the shapes, but both shapes should be approximately the same size.

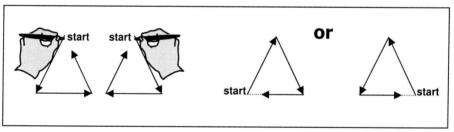

Figure 7.9.3

Materials Needed: Two dry erase markers and a whiteboard
Practice Time: 10-12 shapes per day until the exercise is easily done
Minimum Mastery: The student can duplicate a sequence of strokes moving the dominant and non-dominant hands in opposite directions simultaneously. The student can simultaneously make figures of similar size with the dominant and non-dominant hands.

Processing Goals:
Cross Patterning ~ Can easily use dominant and non-dominant hands simultaneously
Tracking ~ Can make both figures using the same sequence of lines
Direction ~ Can make figures with hands moving in opposite directions

Size ~ Can simultaneously make figures of similar size with the dominant and non-dominant hands

Figure 7.9.4

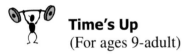 **Time's Up**
(For ages 9-adult)

The parent will set the timer for 20 seconds. The student will then look at the numbers on the timer face, trying to match the rhythm of the countdown. The student will count backwards from 20 to 1 out loud, matching the rhythm of the timer. When this is easily done, the student will match the rhythm of the timer (counting out loud) while not looking at the timer. The student will raise his hand at the moment he anticipates the timer's ring. When this is easily done, the student will say the ABC's or answer questions while making the judgment of time, raising his hand when he anticipates the timer will ring. If the student is saying the ABC's, have him/her start on a different letter each time.

Materials Needed: Digital Timer
Practice Time: Do 3 times per day for 20 seconds
Minimum Mastery: The student can consistently estimate the length of 20 seconds while saying the ABC's or answering questions

Processing Goals:
 Motor Match ~ Can accurately judge time using an auditory rhythm

Figure Ground ~ Can accurately judge time while saying the ABC's or answering questions

Size ~ Can consistently judge the length of 20 seconds

10. Shape: The ability to use all of the mental processes to conceptualize.

Symptoms:
Low comprehension, difficulty understanding math concepts
Physical Shape:
Recognizing patterns
Mental Shape:
Forming details into a concept

The brain processes thousands of bits of information every second of every day. The ability of the brain to process these bits and pieces of information, recognize patterns within this information and form concepts is critical to making appropriate choices and/or responses.

If the student does not recognize appropriate patterns of behavior, he will struggle in his social environment. He will also have difficulty learning from past experiences, as he will not connect adverse consequences to certain types of behavior. Creating structure and consistency in one's life is extremely difficult if the process of Shape is underdeveloped.

In education, the process of Shape helps us put bits and pieces of information together to form concepts. Good math students know more than how to go through the steps to get the correct answer. They understand why it is the correct answer and can duplicate the process in similar problems and apply these math concepts to real life situations to solve problems.

Eric was a sixth grade student who had always struggled with school, particularly math. Eric's mom was single with two other young children. She was extremely busy and often stressed out trying to keep their ship afloat.

Eric was in resource classes for math, which means he was probably two years or more behind. His mother tried to help him, but she was not good at math either. Even with the school and his mother's help, he continued to fall further behind. At great financial sacrifice, she enrolled him in an elite academic testing and tutoring center hoping the extra instruction would make a difference. Over time his math did improve and everyone was excited when he finished at the tutoring center. He wasn't out of resource classes, but math was much easier. As he moved through the seventh grade, new math concepts were introduced. Eric started to struggle again. Each concept had numerous rules to follow, but as before, for Eric the rules and concepts made no sense.

Examples of Activities to Improve Shape

Elements of Shape:

1. The student can identify and follow patterns
2. The student can use characteristics or abilities to categorize
3. The student can use attributes to determine similarities or connections

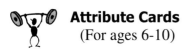 **Attribute Cards**
(For ages 6-10)

The instructor will show the student an attribute card (see Figure 7.10.1). The student will tell the instructor something about the picture without saying the name. The instructor will say, "Tell me something it is or something it does without telling me the name." Example: If the instructor shows the student a picture of an apple, the student could say, "It's red" or "It's good to eat" or "It grows on a tree."

Materials Needed: Attribute cards
Practice Time: Do 4-5 attribute cards per day.
Minimum Mastery: Can name at least three attributes for each card.

Processing Goals:
Cross Patterning ~ Can match meaning with attribute pictures
Shape ~ Can identify attributes and define critical elements

Enlarge to 150% and cut into individual pictures before using

Figure 7.10.1

 Hand Jive 3 Part
(For ages 8-adult)

The instructor will demonstrate the following: Place both hands on the thighs with hands in a fist and fingers down (Figure 7.10.2). The instructor will then raise both hands, rotating the thumbs up and opening the hands while lowering them back to the thighs (Figure 7.10.3). Raise both hands again while rotating the thumbs back to center and lowering outstretched hands to the thighs (Figure 7.10.4). The three movements would be: Fists to the thighs with fingers facing downward, sides of outstretched hands to the thighs, then outstretched hands flat on the thighs. Continue doing the three coordinated hand movements, with smooth, rhythmic movements as quickly as possible. The student will copy the instructor using the same rhythmic movements. When this exercise is mastered, add stress (distractions) by having the student say the ABC's or answer questions.

Materials Needed: None
Practice Time: 1-2 minutes per day until easily done
Minimum Mastery: Can make 12-15 correct movements without stops or hesitations when stress is added.

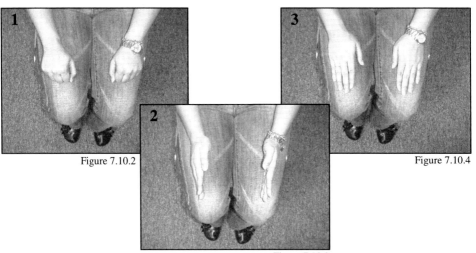

Figure 7.10.2

Figure 7.10.4

Figure 7.10.3

Processing Goals:
Cross Patterning ~ Can easily coordinate both hand movements simultaneously
Tracking ~ Can sequence movements in the correct order
Figure Ground ~ Can make correct movements while being distracted by saying ABC's or answering questions
Shape ~ Can repeat a kinesthetic pattern

 **Hand Jive Crossover**
(For ages 8-adult)

The student will start the exercise with both hands extended out, palms down, with the upper arms close to the body and the lower arms in a horizontal position. (The hands will remain palms down and lower arms extended horizontally for the entire exercise. See Figure 7.10.5.) The student will move the hands in the following sequence of steps:

- Left hand touches the left thigh
- Right hand touches the right thigh
- Raise left hand and move it to the center of the body
- Raise right hand underneath left hand until hands come together (both palms facing down) 12-14 inches above the thighs

The sequence is then repeated beginning with the right hand:

- Right hand touches the right thigh
- Left hand touches the left thigh
- Raise right hand and move it to the center of the body
- Raise left hand underneath right hand until hands come together (both palms facing down) 12-14 inches above the thighs

The exercise is done by continually repeating the two sequences with smooth, rhythmic movements. The student will try to increase the number of consecutive movements done correctly each day. When this is easily done, the instructor can challenge the student to increase the tempo of the rhythm while maintaining correct movements.

Needed Materials: None
Practice Time: 1-2 minutes per day until easily done
Minimum Mastery: Can coordinate all movements in the exercise 10 -12 times using smooth, rhythmic movements without stops or hesitations

Processing Goals:
Cross Patterning ~ Can coordinate hand movements on both sides of the body while crossing the vertical midline

Tracking ~ Can respond with a correct sequence of movements
Shape ~ Can repeat a kinesthetic pattern

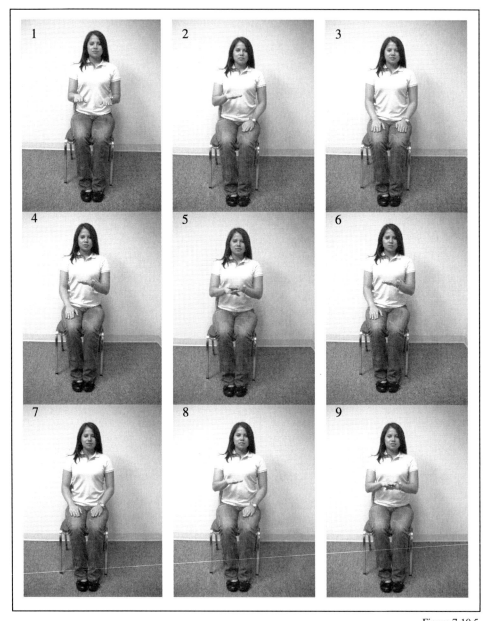

Figure 7.10.5

Summary

The ten preceding examples were simplified for ease in explaining the relationship of the symptoms to the underlying problems. All of the students discussed actually had a number of weaknesses. Almost all struggling students have multiple processing problems that collaborate to produce the symptoms seen by parents and teachers. For example, a student displaying the symptom of poor reading may have problems in one or more of the following skills: visual tracking, visual memory, sound discrimination, concentration and/or processing rhythm. If the student has problems in more than one area, as is usually the case, the detection and treatment of only one of the weaknesses might improve the student's performance to some degree, but total success will be elusive. Finding and treating all the conditions that contribute to a learning disability is a daunting task, but it is something Learning Technics believes is possible.

Neuro-scientists have discovered that the power of the brain grows in direct proportion to the number of connections it has. Researchers are finding that specific mental exercises cause physical changes in the brain that strengthen and increase connections between neuro-processing centers of the brain.

"Science is awakening to the fact that the brain reorganizes itself during learning," said Michael Merzenich (1995), a pioneering neuroscientist at the University of California at San Francisco. "It's something that people don't realize. They don't think about the power that they have within themselves to change their brain."

Learning Technics understands the power within and has developed solutions that can permanently strengthen neuro pathways and help struggling students improve their level of success and enjoy the process of learning.

About the Author

John Heath is CEO of Learning Technics Inc., an applied research company. In 1988 he sensed that the solutions to many learning problems were available–they existed in scores of disciplines waiting to be assembled. "My goal was to find these pieces, and bring them together into a step-by-step program that was highly effective and could be readily dispersed to the many individuals who struggle with learning," Heath explains. He has been on the forefront of converting the most recent neuro-scientific research into practical applications that will permanently improve an individual's ability to learn. He has lectured from Kansas to California in public and private settings. Learning Technics has successfully treated thousands of struggling students in six states, in both public education and the private sector. The Learning Technics Company was recently invited to present its findings at an international conference on learning disabilities at Oxford University. PBS Television aired a documentary covering the research and techniques contained in this book. It can be viewed at LearningTechnics.com

Bibliography

Alvert, M., et al, 1995. "Predictor of cognitive changes in older persons: Mac Arthur studies of successful aging," *Psychology and Aging*, 10: 578-89.

Kalil, R., and P. Lipton. 1995. Neurotrophic factors. Part Two: Their Role in Development, Trauma and Disease. In *Promega Notes 51*, ed. C. Stock, 15-20. Madison, Wisconsin: Promega Corp.

Koslowe, K.C. 1995. Optometric services in a reading disability clinic: Initial results. *Journal of Behavioral Optometry*, 6: 67-68.

Kotulak, Ronald. *Inside the Brain*. Kansas City: Andrews & McMeel, 1996.

McEwen, B.S.. *Stressful Experience, Brain, and Emotion: Behavioral and Neuroendocrine Correlates*. The Cognitive Neuro-sciences, 1117-35. Cambridge, Mass.: MIT Press, 1995.

Merzenich, M. M., and W. M. Jenkins. 1995. Cortical plasticity, learning and learning dysfunction. In *Maturational Windows and Adult Cortical Plasticity Proceedings Vol. 22, Santa Fe Institute, Studies in the Sciences of Complexity*, eds. B. Julez and I. Kovacs, 247-72. New York: Addison-Wesley.

Ramey, Craig T., and Sharon Landsman Ramey, 1992. *At Risk Does Not Mean Doomed*. National Health/Education Consortium Occasional Paper #4.

Restak, Richard M. and Corbin, David. *The Secret Life of the Brain*. United States of America, Dana Press and Joseph Henry Press, 2001.

Sousa, David A. *How the Special Needs Brain Works*. Thousand Oaks, California; Corwin Press, Inc., 2001.

Tallal, P. 1994. "In the perception of speech, time is of the essence," *Temporal Codings in the Brain*, eds. G. Buzsaki, et al., 291-99. Berlin: Springer-Verlag.

INDEX